ONE WAY PENDULUM

ONE WAY PENDULUM

A Farce in a New Dimension

N.F. SIMPSON

faber and faber
LONDON · BOSTON

First published in 1960
by Faber and Faber Limited
3 Queen Square London WC1N 3AU
First published in this edition 1965
Reprinted in 1968, 1972 and 1975
Reissued in 1988

Printed in Great Britain by
Cox & Wyman Ltd, Reading, Berkshire
All rights reserved

All applications for professional and amateur
rights should be addressed to the author via
Faber and Faber Limited 3 Queen Square London WC1N 3AU.

ISBN 0 571 06087 0

To JOYCE

WITH LOVE

The first performance in Great Britain of *One Way Pendulum* was given at the Theatre Royal, Brighton, on 14th December 1959 by the English Stage Company. It was directed by William Gaskill, with décor by Stephen Doncaster and music arranged by Dudley Moore. The cast was as follows:

KIRBY GROOMKIRBY	Roddy Maude-Roxby
ROBERT BARNES	John Horsley
MABEL GROOMKIRBY	Alison Leggatt
SYLVIA GROOMKIRBY	Patsy Rowlands
AUNT MILDRED	Patsy Byrne
MYRA GANTRY	Gwen Nelson
ARTHUR GROOMKIRBY	George Benson
STAN HONEYBLOCK	Douglas Livingstone
JUDGE	Douglas Wilmer
POLICEMAN	Alan Gibson
USHER	Jeremy Longhurst
CLERK OF THE COURT	Robert Levis
PROSECUTING COUNSEL	Graham Crowden
DEFENDING COUNSEL	Graham Armitage

The play was subsequently presented by Ed and David Mirvish at the Royal Alexandra Theatre, Toronto on 26 February 1988 and at The Old Vic, London on 29 April 1988.
The cast was as follows:

KIRBY GROOMKIRBY	Andrew St.Clair
ROBERT BARNES	John Bird
MABEL GROOMKIRBY	Brenda Bruce
SYLVIA GROOMKIRBY	Kathryn Pogson
AUNT MILDRED	Betty Turner
MYRA GANTRY	Ann Way
ARTHUR GROOMKIRBY	Peter Bayliss
STAN HONEYBLOCK	Paul Bigley
JUDGE	Graham Crowden
POLICEMAN	Martin Sadler
USHER	Frank Taylor
CLERK OF THE COURT	John Scarborough
PROSECUTING COUNSEL	John Savident
DEFENDING COUNSEL	John Fortune
Director	Jonathan Miller
Designer	Richard Hudson
Lighting	Bill Wardroper
Administrator	Andrew Leigh

CHARACTERS

KIRBY GROOMKIRBY

has the gauche ungainliness of the self-absorbed introvert. Takes himself very seriously. Only with his weighing machines is he at all relaxed, and remains even then slightly grotesque. Uneasy and querulous in his rare encounters with people. Dressed entirely in black.

ROBERT BARNES

a well-built man in his middle thirties. Has a friendly, casual, confident manner—a police sergeant, perhaps, off-duty. Wears a sports jacket and grey trousers. On neighbourly terms both with the Groomkirbys and the audience. Throws out remarks in an informative, conversational way.

MABEL GROOMKIRBY

a woman of about forty-five. Mother of Kirby Groomkirby. Takes in her stride most of what happens indoors, and is only marginally concerned with anything that may happen elsewhere. Moves briskly and would rather get things done herself than wait for other people to do them.

SYLVIA GROOMKIRBY

daughter of Mabel Groomkirby. Not yet nineteen, but with a permanent air of premature disillusionment about her. Her clothes are casual—neither conventional nor exceptionally bizarre.

AUNT MILDRED

sister of Mabel Groomkirby. A little older than her sister. Her hair and her clothes, which are nondescript, combine to suggest something remote and fey about her in a down-to-earth way. But she is not overtly eccentric.

MYRA GANTRY

> enormously fat through incessant eating in a vocational capacity. She gives her services professionally, but has acquired a somewhat special status in the Groomkirby household through the regularity of her visits.

ARTHUR GROOMKIRBY

> husband of Mabel Groomkirby. He is an ineffectually self-important man in his middle forties, who sets far greater store by being master in his own house than he would if he were. Takes for granted the overriding importance of everything he himself is engaged on.

STANLEY HONEYBLOCK

> looks like a sensible, well-balanced practical young man. A skilled technician of some kind, probably, in a reasonably well-paid job which enables him to dress in a neat and appropriately conventional way, when he comes to take Sylvia out. Good-natured, unpretentious.

IN THE LAW COURT:

JUDGE

> A taller man than Arthur Groomkirby, and slightly older. He is unhurried, sure of himself, and with the instincts— sublimated by his profession—of a stoat.

PROSECUTING COUNSEL

> thrusting, relentless, slightly sadistic—but using as a weapon an elaborate pretence of casual, supercilious indifference.

DEFENDING COUNSEL

> seedy, bumbling, sentimental, well-meaning. Older than the prosecuting counsel, but conscious of being less effectual —hence very determined.

USHER   CLERK OF THE COURT   POLICEMAN

ACT ONE

The GROOMKIRBYS' living-room.
A door Back opens inwards. Part of a kitchen can
be seen through it.
A door Right opens inwards giving a view of the
hall, and part of the staircase.
Against the wall Right, and Right of this door,
stands a cash register, covered and so
unrecognizable.
Leading inconspicuously up the wall from the cash
register is a tube which disappears into the
ceiling.
The fireplace is on the left. On the mantelpiece
above it, almost lost among other oddments, stands
a small replica of a skull, where a clock might
normally be.
A table, with a chair by it, is covered with papers
and large black books. These also are to be seen
filling a bookshelf, and scattered about the room.
There is the usual furniture in addition, including
an armchair, a sideboard downstage Left, and a
wall mirror.
*When the curtain rises the stage is in darkness. The
light comes slowly up on three centrally placed
weighing machines.*
*Number One, in the middle, is large and eye-
catching and flamboyantly ugly. On it is an
enormous weight.*
*Number Two, on the right, and Number Three, on
the left, are identically small, modest, unpretentious.
On them are correspondingly smaller weights.*
Pause.
KIRBY *enters with a music stand which he places*

centrally opposite Number One. He adjusts its
height. There is no music on it.
As KIRBY *takes up his baton and adopts an*
appropriate stance, the light contracts to isolate
Number One.

KIRBY: (*on one note*). Mi mi mi mi mi mi mi mi mi mi
mi mi mi.
He listens coaxingly. Silence. He tries again.
Pause.

NUMBER ONE: (*metallic, mechanical voice*). Mi mi mi mi mi mi
mi mi mi mi mi mi mi.
Kirby repeats the sound a tone higher.
Short pause.
Number One repeats it as before.
Kirby raises the sound another tone.

NUMBER ONE: (*imitating*). Mi mi mi mi . . . (*pause*) . . . Fifteen
stone ten pounds.
Kirby makes an impatient gesture and repeats the
sound on the same note as before.
Pause.

NUMBER ONE: Fifteen stone ten pounds.
Dismissively Kirby taps the music stand and beckons
to Number Two.
Light comes up on Number Two and goes down on
Number One.

KIRBY: (*baton raised. Confident.*) Doh me soh doh[1] soh.

NUMBER TWO: (*sweet soprano*). Doh me soh doh[1] soh.
This is repeated antiphonally several times,
acquiring a kind of jaunty, flirtatious rhythm until,
suddenly recollecting himself, Kirby pulls it up
short by two sharp taps on the music stand.
At this signal the light comes up on Number Three,
leaving Number One visible but in shadow.

KIRBY: Doh me soh doh[1]soh.
He beckons to Number Two.

KIRBY: ⎰ (*an octave higher*)
NUMBER TWO: ⎱ Doh me soh doh[1] soh.
He beckons Number Three with the baton.

KIRBY:
NUMBER TWO:
NUMBER THREE: } *(Number Three sings in a fruity baritone, an octave lower than Kirby)* Doh me soh doh^1 soh.

This is repeated firmly twice. Kirby now fixes his attention sternly on Number One. Light contracts to isolate Number One which is very strongly lit.

KIRBY: *(leaning forward. Forcefully.)* Mi mi mi mi mi mi mi mi mi mi mi mi mi.

Silence. Kirby repeats this twice, trying each time to coax a response but without success. He drops his arms to his side and walks a few steps away from the music stand in despair. The light begins to fade on Number One.

NUMBER ONE: *(just before becoming obliterated).* Fifteen stone ten pounds.

Barnes materializes downstage Right and stands looking on. With sudden decision Kirby returns to the music stand and gives two sharp taps. Light comes up on Number Two and Number Three.

BARNES: Works like a slave on this. Every night. As soon as he gets in.

KIRBY: *(baton poised).* Doh^1. *(Very rapidly.)* Doh^1 doh^1 doh^1 doh^1 doh^1 doh^1 doh^1 doh^1 doh^1. Doh^1

NUMBER TWO:
NUMBER THREE: } Doh^1 me soh doh^1 soh la doh^1 soh fa me doh doh ti doh.

Pause.

BARNES: It's a form of escape, of course. Escapism.

Projected on to a screen behind are about a score of weighing machines in two rows. These swell the density of the sound but the volume is reduced. All except Number One sing.

ALL: *(at a signal from Kirby. Muted.)* Doh me soh doh^1 soh la doh^1 soh: fa me doh doh ti doh.

Pause.

BARNES: He's got big ideas eventually. Massed choirs and that sort of thing.

Kirby taps more peremptorily on the music stand. Two more rows of weighing machines appear. They

launch, full-throatedly, into the Hallelujah Chorus.
Kirby rises magnificently to the occasion and
conducts them with splendid panache.

CHOIR: Ha . . . llelujah!

Six more rows of weighing machines appear.

CHOIR: Ha . . . llelujah!

Another dozen rows.

CHOIR: Hallelujah. Hallelujah.

Countless weighing machines as far as the eye can see.

CHOIR: (*a glorious avalanche of sound*). Ha . . . a . . . llelu
. . . u . . . jah!

Kirby, after the sound has died away and as the
vista fades, stands transfixed in triumphant ecstasy
with arms outstretched.

BARNES: (*nonchalantly*). Delusions of grandeur they call it,
don't they?

The vision fades, the light contracts and at last
only Number One is visible.

NUMBER ONE: (*metallic and mechanical as ever*). Fifteen stone ten
pounds.

Kirby deflates slowly but perceptibly. Fade Out.
Isolated in two pools of light are Barnes, who is
still downstage Right, and Mrs. Groomkirby, who
is at the open drawer of the sideboard downstage Left.

BARNES: (*on Fade Out*). Good long way to go yet.

MRS. G.: (*looking sharply round*). What?

BARNES: (*gesturing upwards*). Hallo, Mrs. Groomkirby. I
was just talking about Kirby up there.

MRS. G.: (*reverting to the drawer*). Oh, it's you, Mr. Barnes.
I wondered who it was.

BARNES: Won't have to worry about hiring the Wembley
Stadium, just yet awhile.

MRS. G.: (*without looking round*). Still having trouble with
Brother Gormless up there, is he?

BARNES: Running his head up against a brick wall there, if
you ask me.

MRS. G.: The whole thing's ridiculous. Why he can't use
records . . .

BARNES: The lazy man's way, Mrs. Groomkirby. Besides—
you don't know what's behind it.

MRS. G.: (*closing drawer and opening another*). No. Neither
does anybody else. I don't think he knows himself.

BARNES: Wait till he's got all five hundred of them up to
concert pitch!

MRS. G.: Well, as far as that goes, if we've got to *have* five
hundred weighing machines in the house, I'd just
as soon they did sing. Especially if they've got
nothing more to say for themselves than Gormless.

BARNES: True enough.

MRS. G.: 'Fifteen stone ten' all day long—it gets a bit
monotonous after a time.

BARNES: I should imagine it does. (*Pause.*) Is it all right if
we come in, by the way?

MRS. G.: (*looking sharply at Barnes and then suspiciously
into the Auditorium*). If who come in?

BARNES: Unless you'd rather we went off and came back
later?
*Mrs. Groomkirby gives Barnes a meaningful glance
and, closing the drawer, starts tidying things on top
of the sideboard.*

MRS. G.: Like living on the pavement!
Pause.

BARNES: I'll bring them in, then, shall I, Mrs. Groomkirby?

MRS. G.: Yes. I suppose they'd better come in if they're
coming.
*As Mrs. Groomkirby briskly passes into the room the
light follows her and comes up over the whole room.
She picks up papers and other oddments in her
passage towards the door into the kitchen.
As the light comes up the phone rings in the hall.*

MRS. G.: There's the phone, Sylvia. (*To Barnes without
looking round.*) They'll have to take it as they find
it. I haven't got time to go round scrubbing and
polishing for them. (*She goes out into the kitchen
leaving the door open.*)

15

BARNES: Oh, no, they won't expect anything like that. *Sylvia has been sitting languidly in the armchair reading a magazine. She gets up with a marked lack of enthusiasm and crosses to the door into the hall. As she opens it Kirby's voice can be heard singing 'Mi mi mi mi . . .', and this is repeated in metallic tones. Sylvia goes out leaving the door slightly open.*

SYLVIA: (*off. In a bored, disenchanted voice.*) Yes?

BARNES: (*gently closing the door on the inside behind Sylvia and at the same time cutting off the sound. With a nod upwards.*) Still at it. (*Moving casually towards the table in the middle of the room.*) He's just above here. He's got the room over this one. *He approaches the table, which is littered with books and papers, and in a mildly inquisitive way begins glancing at titles.*

BARNES: (*as an afterthought*). This is the living-room, of course. (*More loudly.*) Where's Arthur this evening, Mrs. Groomkirby?

MRS. G.: (*off*). Need you ask?

BARNES: Across at the library again, I suppose?

MRS. G.: (*off*). I wonder he doesn't take his bed there and have done with it.

BARNES: (*to audience. Informatively.*) Mr. Groomkirby. He makes a bit of a hobby of the law. Gets a lot of books out of the library and one thing and another. They're all legal books—all this lot. (*Reading out titles.*) 'Every man His Own Lawyer'. 'Legal Procedure for the Layman'. (*He drifts across to the bookshelf.*) Actually he's an insurance agent or something, I believe, when he's working. There's some more of them over here. This is his great hobby at the moment.

MRS. G.: (*entering to put something in a drawer*). Hobby. I don't know about a hobby. (*Going out.*) He spends more time on that than he does on anything else.

BARNES: (*taking down a book that has caught his eye and thumbing through it*). Gets a bit single-minded about it at times, doesn't he?

MRS. G.: (*off*). Cluttering the place up. What with Kirby upstairs and him down. Never speaking to each other from one week's end to the next.

BARNES: (*putting the book back and running his finger along the titles*). 'Perjury for Pleasure'. 'Out and About on Circuit'. 'Teach Yourself Torts'. (*He stops short at a title.*) *Cabinet* making? (*He looks in an intensely puzzled way in the vague direction of the audience and then back at the shelf.*) What does *he* want with a book on cabinet making? 'The Complete Cabinet Maker and Joiner'. 'Do's and Don't's for Dovetailers'. 'Ways With Wood'. What's going on? (*Loudly.*) He's not taking up carpentry now, is he? As well?

MRS. G.: (*appearing at door*). Who?

BARNES: Arthur. He's got enough books here on it. There's another one down here—'Noah's Ark: The Supreme Achievement in Wood'. What's he up to, Mrs. Groomkirby?

MRS. G.: (*going*). Don't ask me. Something else for me to dust, I expect, whatever it is.

BARNES: (*moving downstage Left*). Well, if he's got ideas about building Noah's Ark in a room this size, he'll find he's bitten off a bit more than he can chew.

MRS. G.: (*off*). As long as we don't have to be knee-deep in shavings while he's finding out.

BARNES: I shouldn't worry too much. It probably doesn't amount to anything, Mrs. Groomkirby. I just happened to see them there. He's probably had them for years.

MRS. G.: (*entering with wheelchair as Sylvia enters from hall, letting in the sound momentarily of Kirby's singing lesson, which is cut off abruptly as she closes door again*). He's seen them lying about somewhere

and picked them up thinking he'd got hold of
something else. He doesn't know what day it is
half the time.

*Mrs. Groomkirby places the wheelchair downstage
Left in the position it quite clearly occupies regularly.
In it is Aunt Mildred. She sits placidly gazing at
the floor some ten feet in front of her. Mrs. Groomkirby settles Aunt Mildred in an impersonal,
businesslike way, and then crosses the room to get a
large coloured travel brochure to bring to Aunt
Mildred. Sylvia has crossed without a word to the
armchair and thrown herself down in it to look
again at her magazine.*

BARNES: (*leaning against the edge of the seat quite close to
Aunt Mildred. Aside to audience with nod towards
Aunt Mildred.*) Aunt Mildred. (*Pause.*) Never
think they were sisters, would you?

*Mrs. Groomkirby returns with the travel brochure
and puts it on Aunt Mildred's lap unceremoniously
in passing like a waitress putting a menu on a table.*

BARNES: (*with a nod*). Travel brochure.

MRS. G.: (*going briskly out to kitchen. Without looking at
Sylvia.*) Who was that?

SYLVIA: (*without looking up*). Stan.
Pause.

BARNES: (*half to himself, half to audience. Shaking his head
dubiously.*) Noah's Ark in *there*! I hope he knows
what he's doing.
Pause. He begins to move off Left.

AUNT M.: (*quoting indignantly from brochure*). 'By rail to
Outer Space!' And here I am sitting here.
Barnes checks.

BARNES: (*with a sly glance at the audience. Very slightly
humouring her.*) Perhaps you got on the wrong
train, Aunt Mildred.

AUNT M.: Of course I was on the wrong train. I knew the
moment I heard the man say Outer Hebrides that
I was on the wrong train.

BARNES: She's got this bug about transport. Wants us all moving about. Don't you, Aunt Mildred? Plenty of destinations—so we can feel as if we're getting somewhere. She's probably right. Nothing like a good old destination for giving you a sense of purpose. Till you get there, of course. Then you have to start looking round for another one. That's why you need plenty *of* them. Can't have too many, can you, Aunt Mildred? (*No reply.*) Too wrapped up in her brochure. (*Moving off Left.*) Just want to slip upstairs for a moment. I'll be back in a minute.
Barnes goes off.
Pause.
Mrs. Groomkirby enters briefly to put something away.
MRS. G.: (*without looking at Sylvia*). I thought you weren't seeing Stan any more.
SYLVIA: (*without looking up*). I didn't say I *was* seeing him.
MRS. G.: (*disappearing through the door*). As long as you don't expect *me* to be all over him when he comes.
Pause. Mrs. Groomkirby enters with a tray on which a snack is laid out.
MRS. G.: (*putting the tray down*). Here you are, Sylvia. If you're not doing anything you can take this upstairs to Kirby.
Sylvia looks momentarily up and goes back to the magazine.
Mrs. Groomkirby begins clearing Mr. Groomkirby's books and papers off the table.
Short pause.
SYLVIA: Can't he come down for it himself?
MRS. G.: You know very well he's busy up there.
Mrs. Groomkirby briskly completes the clearing of the table with no respect at all for the books or papers, which she puts unceremoniously in a corner, and goes out to the kitchen.
MRS. G.: (*going and indicating tray*). Don't let that get cold, Sylvia.

SYLVIA: (*stirring herself reluctantly*). Why can't he get records or something and play those—like anybody else? Instead of this everlasting mi mi mi mi all the damn time.

Sylvia takes up the tray and makes for the door into the hall.

SYLVIA: I suppose that's something else that's against his principles. He'd rather go through all this pantomime. (*Opening door. Sound of singing lesson.*) Listen to it!

MRS. G.: (*off*). It's only until he gets them all trained properly, Sylvia.

SYLVIA: (*closing the door behind her and cutting off the sound*). Gets them trained! I can't wait! (*Re-opening door.*) Then, I suppose, we shall have Handel's Messiah driving us all up the wall every time there's anything on the telly. (*She closes door.*)

Mrs. Groomkirby comes in and out during the following dialogue to put food on the table. She lays a place for one but the food is enough for ten. Pause. Mrs. Groomkirby enters briefly.

AUNT M.: What's happened to my tricycle, Mabel?

MRS. G.: (*going out*). You know perfectly well it hasn't come yet, Aunt Mildred.

Pause.

AUNT M.: I shall be too old to ride it if it doesn't come soon.

Pause.

AUNT M.: (*loudly to Mrs. Groomkirby*). Do you remember the trouble Maud had with that tricycle of hers, Mabel?

Pause. Mrs. Groomkirby enters.

AUNT M.: She went by bus in the end.

Pause.

AUNT M.: It didn't take her long to change from one to the other. She never stuck to anything for any length of time. Wheelbarrows, roller skates, rickshaws— I think she's tried practically everything at one time or another.

Mrs. Groomkirby goes out.

AUNT M.: I can remember when it was camels. (*Loudly.*) Do you remember that, Mabel? I can remember the time when she wouldn't go anywhere without her camel. If she wasn't up on top of it she was walking along beside it.

Pause.

AUNT M.: She rode to hounds on it more than once.

Pause.

AUNT M.: Until it threw her. Then she went on to roller skates.

Pause.

AUNT M.: Now it's buses. She wouldn't hear a word at one time against that camel. 'My ship of the desert' she used to say. But not any longer. Not since it threw her.

Pause.

AUNT M.: I told her they were treacherous. But she wouldn't listen.

Pause.

AUNT M.: She was perfectly all right till the police stopped her that time with Dr. Picklock's ambulance.

Pause.

AUNT M.: Do you remember that, Mabel? In the middle of the night.

MRS. G.: (*speaking as she crosses the kitchen past the open door but without looking in*). She was committing a nuisance with it, Aunt Mildred.

Pause.

AUNT M.: It was only through the kindness of Dr. Picklock that she had an ambulance to commit a nuisance with.

Pause. Mrs. Groomkirby crosses back.

AUNT M.: In any case it was empty.

Mrs. Groomkirby enters, speaking impatiently but without looking at Aunt Mildred.

MRS.G. We know it was empty, Aunt Mildred. But she knocked down Dr. Picklock with it

Pause. Mrs. Groomkirby busies herself with the table.

AUNT M.: (*as Mrs. Groomkirby is about to go out*). Knocked down a doctor? With an ambulance? How could she? It's a contradiction in terms!

MRS. G.: (*checking and turning to look for the first time straight at Aunt Mildred's back. In angry impatience.*) He was six weeks in *plaster*, Aunt Mildred!

As Mrs. Groomkirby turns and goes out, Sylvia enters from the hall. Brief sound of singing lesson. Mrs. Groomkirby checks momentarily and then continues out.

SYLVIA: (*closing door and crossing to armchair*). Listen to it out there! It's going to drive me up the wall before long.

MRS. G.: (*off*). For goodness' sake don't *you* start, Sylvia.

SYLVIA: (*sitting with magazine*). Mi mi mi mi-ing all over the place. He's been on it now since I don't know when and he still isn't any further.

MRS. G.: (*off*). He's got to go at the pace of the slowest. You know that, Sylvia, as well as I do.

SYLVIA: He's got four hundred and ninety-nine others for goodness' sake! He doesn't have to hold everything up just for the sake of Gormless! If he goes at the pace of Gormless he'll still be mi mi mi-ing in six months' time.

MRS. G.: (*off*). That's Kirby's affair, Sylvia. I've got quite enough to do down here moving your father's stuff about all over the place before I can get on with anything—without bothering about what Kirby's doing or isn't doing. (*Pause.*) If *you* gave a hand now and again it might be a help. (*Pause.*) What with you moaning and Aunt Mildred on all the time.

SYLVIA: Why? What's wrong with her?

MRS. G.: (*off*). Nothing Don't for heaven's sake start her off. *Pause.*

SYLVIA: I don't know what she's doing there in the first place.

MRS. G.: (*entering with food*). You know perfectly well she got on the wrong train, Sylvia.

SYLVIA: Cluttering up the place.

MRS. G.: We're not getting rid of her. If that's what you're leading up to. We've been over this before.

SYLVIA: Great old-fashioned thing in the living-room.

MRS. G.: Yes. Well, she's staying where she is. (*Pause. (Going out to kitchen*). Did you ring Kirby's bell when you came down? Because I didn't hear it if you did.
Sylvia throws down the magazine in exasperation and getting up crosses to the cash register.

SYLVIA: I don't know what he wants a bell rung every time for.

MRS. G.: (*off*). You know he won't start eating till he's heard it.

SYLVIA: (*uncovering the cash register*). What happens when this thing wears out? That's what I want to know. (*Pausing with fingers poised over the keys.*) What is it—No Sale?

MRS. G.: (*off*). Surely you know by now, Sylvia. Yes.

SYLVIA: Starve to death, I suppose. (*Ringing up No Sale.*) He was perfectly all right till he heard about Pavlov and those stupid dogs. (*Covering the cash register and returning to armchair, but checking on passing the table as though noticing it for the first time.*) What's all this for, mum, for goodness' sake? Not Mrs. Gantry again?

MRS. G.: (*off*). Somebody's got to eat the food up, Sylvia.

SYLVIA: (*sitting*). Oh, no! Not her *again*!

MRS. G.: (*off*). It's no use leaving it to mount up. I've only got the one larder, Sylvia.

SYLVIA: Couldn't she have come some other night? She would have to be here on the one night I've got Stan coming

MRS. G.: (*appearing at the door* and looking *pointedly in*

23

Sylvia's direction for a moment before speaking). I
thought you weren't seeing Stan.

SYLVIA: Trust her to choose tonight of all nights!
*Mrs. Groomkirby says nothing. She goes back into
the kitchen.*
Pause.

SYLVIA: What time's she going to be here?

MRS. G.: (*entering with food*). I don't know, Sylvia.

SYLVIA: It's eight o'clock now gone. Stan's supposed to
be coming at quarter past nine.

MRS. G.: You haven't got to both sit there and watch her,
have you?

SYLVIA: What are we supposed to do then?

MRS. G.: If you were to do your proper share of the eating
between you, instead of leaving it all to me, I
shouldn't have to have Mrs. Gantry in anything
like so often. (*Pause.*) Paying out good money all
the time. (*Pause.*) If it weren't for your father's
parking meters we just shouldn't be able to run
to it. Then we should *have* to get it eaten ourselves.

AUNT M.: Twenty-five years since I left St. Pancras . . .

MRS. G.: Be quiet, Aunt Mildred!

AUNT M.: . . . and here I am still sitting here.

MRS. G.: It's all very well for you, Sylvia, to sit there
carrying on. It's your father who has to stand out
there hour after hour in all weathers to try and
get enough together to pay the bills with. (*Pause.*)
If you don't want to stay in, there's nothing to
stop you going out, is there? You're not going to
sit there saying nothing all the evening, both of
you, are you?

SYLVIA: I don't know what we're going to do yet. If she's
coming we haven't got much choice. I can't take
him upstairs with the Mastersingers going full
blast up there, can I?

MRS.G. (*checking*). No, you certainly can't, Sylvia! And
while we're about it let's get one thing clear. I

24

don't mind Stan coming here. As long as he's not under *my* feet all the time. But we can get one thing settled here and now—he's not being taken upstairs. That's quite definite.

AUNT M.: It isn't at all how I envisaged it, Mabel.

MRS. G.: (*reverting to table*). That's one thing I do draw the line at. (*Pause.*) (*Going out to kitchen with a glance in passing at the mantelpiece.*) If that's yours on the mantelpiece, Sylvia, you might put it away somewhere before Mrs. Gantry gets here. *Sylvia glances up momentarily and goes on reading. Pause.*

AUNT M.: Not even a luggage rack for my things, Mabel.

SYLVIA: She's off again, mum.

MRS. G.: (*off*). For goodness' sake leave her alone. I can hear she is. *Pause.*

AUNT M.: It hardly seems like travelling. (*Pause.*) I wouldn't mind if I could feel I were moving towards something.

MRS. G.: (*entering and answering the earlier point about luggage racks*). You can hardly *expect* to have a luggage rack in the Outer Hebrides, Aunt Mildred.

SYLVIA: Pity she can't *be* in the Outer Hebrides. *Pause.*

A series of regular thuds as of someone rolling a heavy angular weight across the floor overhead is heard.

Mrs. Groomkirby looks up, then across at Sylvia, who does not react in any way at all, then briefly up again before reverting with a resigned sigh to what she was doing before. Pause.

MRS. G.: (*going*). You haven't done anything about that yet, have you, Sylvia? It isn't exactly an ornament to have about the place.

SYLVIA Why? What's wrong with it? It's only a death's head.

25

MRS. G.: (*off*). A dirty old skull on the mantelpiece. (*Pause.*) (*Entering.*) I should have thought you could have found something better to do with your money than spend it on a thing like that.

SYLVIA: As a matter of fact, it's a memento mori, if you really want to know.

MRS. G.: Oh? And what's a memento mori for heaven's sake?

SYLVIA: Stan bought it for me. You carry it round with you.

MRS. G.: It looks like it. Stuck up there.

SYLVIA: You don't *have* to carry it round. As long as it's somewhere where you can see it. It's supposed to remind you of death.
There is an eloquent pause.

MRS. G.: And does it?

SYLVIA: (*looking up*). Does it what?

MRS. G.: (*without looking round*). I thought it was supposed to remind you of death.

SYLVIA: (*shrugging*). Oh. (*Glancing at skull and going back to magazine.*) Not all that much.
Pause.

MRS. G.: (*going out into kitchen*). I think you'd better tell Stan he's been done over that, then, Sylvia.
Sylvia affects indifference and goes on reading.
Pause.
A second series of thuds, slightly louder and slightly slower, as though the weight this time were a heavier one.
Pause.

AUNT M.: If only I could feel I had a proper destination! (*Pause.*) And proper transport to take me there.

SYLVIA: Oh for goodness' sake shut her up, mum!

MRS. G.: (*off*). Be quiet and leave her alone, Sylvia!
Pause.
Mrs. Groomkirby enters briefly.

AUNT M.: We should be a very static lot without any transport to take us from one destination to another.

MRS. G.: (*in desperation*). We don't have to be obsessed with it, Aunt Mildred! (*Mrs. Groomkirby goes out into the kitchen.*)
Long pause.
A third series of thuds, louder and slower, is heard.

MRS. G.: (*appearing at kitchen door*). What's he up to?

SYLVIA: For goodness' sake stop fussing! He's only moving his weights about.

MRS. G.: (*crossing to door into hall*). He'll be rupturing himself up there.
Mrs. Groomkirby opens the door. As she does so the lights in the room go down and Mrs. Groomkirby is seen by the light from the hall outside, standing in the doorway and looking up the stairs. The thuds have become slightly louder through the open door.

MRS. G.: (*calling*). Are you all right, Kirby?
The light in the hall quickly fades out. At the same time Kirby appears downstage Left. He crosses from Left to Right rolling a heavy angular wight as large as himself over and over and goes off.

MRS. G.: (*heard off*). I suppose he's all right.
As the weight disappears off stage a final louder thud is heard.
Short pause.
The sound of a small, male voice choir is heard rather self-consciously singing Rock-a-Bye Baby. Kirby reappears downstage Right and retreats backward from Right to Left conducting imaginary singers with his baton. He disappears off stage on the words 'Down Will Come Baby and Cradle and All'.
Short pause. A reverberating crash.
Short pause.

NUMBER ONE: (*off. In the familiar tones*). Fifteen stone ten pounds.
Light up on living-room.
Mrs. Groomkirby has appeared, alarmed and uncertain for the moment, at the kitchen door

27

MRS. G.: (*suddenly recollecting herself, seizing a cloth and wiping her hands with it as she crosses to the door into the hall*). Don't just sit there, Sylvia!

SYLVIA: He's only knocked his weights down.
Short pause.

SYLVIA: (*as Mrs. Groomkirby is going out into the hall*). Or tripped over them or something.
Mrs. Groomkirby checks and turns back into the room.

MRS. G.: He's probably waiting up there to fall back unconscious.
She goes to the cash register, tears off the cover and throws it down, and rings up No Sale.
A sharp single thud is heard.

MRS. G.: (*rushing out and upstairs*). I thought as much.

NUMBER ONE: (*off*). Fifteen stone ten pounds.
Long pause.

AUNT M.: Four hundred and seventy-nine destinations and not so much as a tricycle to take me to one of them!
Long pause.
Barnes reappears (casually) downstage Left.

BARNES: Everything under control? (*Noticing the door into the hall is open.*) What's happened to the music?
Mrs. Groomkirby comes downstairs and into the room, closing the door behind her.

MRS. G.: (*crossing to kitchen*). He's lying there stunned.
Barnes tries, puzzled, to pick up the lost threads.

MRS. G.: (*off*). It won't hurt him to stay there for a little while. The rest might do him good.
Sound of doorbell. Very short pause.
Mrs. Groomkirby enters and crosses briskly to the door into the hall.

MRS. G.: (*with heavy sarcasm*). Don't bother to answer it, Sylvia, will you?

SYLVIA: (*as Mrs. Groomkirby goes out, leaving the door open*). If that's Mrs. Gantry, mum, I shall be out here washing some things through.

She goes languidly out into the kitchen, closing the
door. Barnes reacts strongly to the name Gantry.
He turns to take down an outdoor coat from a hook
offstage.

BARNES: (*confidentially*). I think perhaps this is where we'll
quietly scarper. Before we get caught. (*Getting into*
outdoor coat.) We'll go outside and have a breather
for a minute or two . . .

MRS. G.: (*off*). Hello, Myra.

MRS. GANTRY: (*off*). I hope I'm not too early, Mabel?

MRS. G.: (*off*). Of course not, Myra. Let me hang that up
here for you.

BARNES: (*crossing rapidly from Left to Right*). Come on.
(*As he passes in front of Aunt Mildred.*) Excuse us,
Aunt Mildred. We're leaving you to it for a little
while.

MRS. G.: (*at door*). I've got everything set out ready for you.

BARNES: (*checking. He is off the set downstage Right*). Here
she is. The fifteen stone wonder.
Mrs. Gantry comes in followed by Mrs. Groomkirby.

MRS. G.: (*pushing back, as she passes it, the drawer of the*
cash register, which she previously left open). We're
just waiting for the kettle.

NUMBER ONE: (*off. As though in response to the slight ping from*
the cash register.) Fifteen stone ten pounds.
Mrs. Gantry checks in surprise which has begun to
turn to indignation when the lights quickly fade and
go up again on a street scene drop showing a
corner house.

BARNES: I stand corrected.
Pause.
Barnes begins rolling a cigarette.

BARNES: I should have told you about the cash register.
Communicates with Kirby's room up there. (*He*
gestures vaguely towards one of the upper windows.)
Don't ask me why. They've got some crack-
brained ideas in that house. He has to have a bell
rung before he can eat anything. He's trained

himself. Conditioned reflex or something. Why it
has to be a cash register God only knows.
Anything with a bell on it would have done just
as well as long as he's got something he can
respond to. Doorbell as far as that goes. All it
wants is for someone to run a lead up to his
room—wouldn't take more than a few minutes.
I'd suggest doing it myself only they're a bit
funny about letting anybody in on it from outside.
They generally keep it covered up actually. I'm
surprised it wasn't covered just now. . . .
*Barnes breaks off, cigarette poised half-way to his
lips, and stares in amazement as a small hand-
cart comes on from Left. It is stacked precariously
with oak panelling.*
*Barnes watches it well on to the stage in its progress
across from Left to Right.*
Pushing it is Mr. Groomkirby.

BARNES: Hold it! (*He darts forward to steady the load.*)

MR. G.: (*peering round the load and seeing Barnes*). Oh, it's
you, Bob, is it? Wondered who it was.

BARNES: What's it all in aid of?

MR. G.: I've been an hour and a half with this lot. (*He
starts pushing again.*) Getting it up here. Traffic
lights and what not.

BARNES: Wait! (*He retrieves a piece of panelling.*) You've got
about twice as much on here as you can manage.
(*Pause.*) There. Try that.

MR. G.: (*moving off*). Oak. Good, solid stuff.

BARNES: (*watching him off*). You're not thinking of trying
to get that whatever it is set up indoors, are you,
by any chance?

MR. G.: Why not?

BARNES: Good God! She'll have a fit!
*He shakes his head after Mr. Groomkirby
despairingly.*

BARNES: (*calling*). Look out! (*Pause.*) You nearly lost the
lot then.

30

MR. G.: (*off*). It's all right. I've only got to get it round the back now.

BARNES: You should have made two journeys with it.

MR. G.: (*off*). No, I didn't want to do that. I just made the one journey and went the long way round. It's as broad as it's long.

As Barnes crosses to the right the drop quickly rises on the living-room where Mrs. Groomkirby and Mrs. Gantry are in conversation.

Mrs. Gantry is sitting at the table where her ravages are already apparent. Mrs. Groomkirby is ironing.

MRS. G.: (*as drop rises*). They go round in circles with it.

MRS. GANTRY: Of course they do.

Barnes cautiously backs out of their line of vision. Pause.

MRS. G.: It's the same with his parking meters.

MRS. GANTRY: Like Mr. Gantry with his.

BARNES: (*aside*). I think I'll just go round and see what's going on out at the back. (*Withdrawing, with a gesture into the room.*) Good luck to you! (*He goes.*)

MRS. G.: Five of them altogether he's got out there, in different places. Round the lawn and up by the rockery. But once he's put his sixpence in there's no budging him. He'll stand there like a statue till his hour's up.

MRS. GANTRY: Mr. Gantry generally takes a book out there with him.

MRS. G.: Instead of going away after he's stood there for ten minutes or so and having sixpenn'orth in front of one of the others. What's the good of *having* five? And the consequence is, of course, that when he goes round to empty them all at the end of the month he's got practically nothing to show for hours of waiting. And he's out in all weathers.

MRS. GANTRY: It's the only way they can save anything.

MRS. G.: He's afraid of anything that's got the least suggestion of overcharging about it. Unless he gets his full hour once he's put his sixpence in he feels he's been done in some way. He's frightened he'll end up losing his own custom.

MRS. GANTRY: If you don't speculate you don't accumulate.

MRS. G.: I tell him, by the time it came to losing his own custom—if it ever did—he could have made enough overcharging himself to pay somebody to stand in front of them twenty-four hours a day. And make his fortune practically. But he can't seem to see it.

MRS. GANTRY: They don't, Mabel. Once they get an idea in their heads. (*Pause.*) You've still got your Aunt Mildred, I see.

MRS. G.: She's in the Outer Hebrides. Waiting for a train back to St. Pancras.
Pause.

MRS. GANTRY: She lives for her transport, doesn't she?

MRS. G.: We're trying to get a tricycle for her—but they don't seem to make them side-saddle any more.
Long pause.

MRS. GANTRY: You heard about Mr. Gridlake?

MRS. G.: No?

MRS. GANTRY: I thought you might have heard. Had an accident on his skis.

MRS. G.: Serious?

MRS. GANTRY: Killed himself.

MRS. G.: No!

MRS. GANTRY: Straight into the jaws of death, so Mrs. Honey-block was saying.
Pause.

MRS. G.: What on earth did he expect to find in there, for goodness sake?

MRS. GANTRY: Showing off, I suppose.
Pause.

MRS. G.: You'd think he'd have had more sense.
Pause.

MRS. GANTRY: He hadn't intended staying there, of course.
Pause.

32

MRS. G.: In one side and out the other, I suppose.

MRS. GANTRY: That's why he had his skis on sideways, according to Mrs. Honeyblock.
Pause.

MRS. G.: I can't think what possessed him.

MRS. GANTRY: Trying to take death in by putting his skis on the wrong way round!
Pause.

MRS. GANTRY: I feel sorry for Mrs. Gridlake.

MRS. G.: What actually happened in there? Missed his footing, I suppose?

MRS. GANTRY: I'll tell you what *I* think happened, Mabel.

MRS. G.: Too confident.

MRS. GANTRY: No. What I think happened was that he went in all right and then caught his head a glancing blow as he was coming out. (*Pause.*) It's easily done. Especially a tall man.

MRS. G.: Stunned himself.

MRS. GANTRY: Stunned himself, and then of course it was too late.
Pause.

MRS. G.: Instead of *allowing* for his height.

MRS. GANTRY: Allow for it? I don't suppose he even knew what it was.

MRS. G.: (*in remonstrance*). Oh! But he must have done! I can't believe he didn't know his own height, Myra.

MRS. GANTRY: Mr. Gantry doesn't.

MRS. G.: Do you mean to say he doesn't know how tall he is?

MRS. GANTRY: He's not all that certain how short he is, Mabel, if it comes to that.

MRS. G.: It's about time you made him have himself measured, Myra.

MRS. GANTRY: The same with his weight. He has to work it out every time.
Pause. Mrs. Groomkirby maintains a silence of disapprobation.

MRS. GANTRY: I didn't tell you about the summer before last, did I? When he went over the edge at Scarborough?

MRS. G.: No?

MRS. GANTRY: Yes—he fell off one of the cliffs playing dominoes with the children.

MRS. G.: I never knew that.

MRS. GANTRY: How long do you think it took him to get to the bottom?

Mrs. Groomkirby looks inquiringly.

MRS. GANTRY: Three hours!

MRS. G.: No!

MRS. GANTRY: All but five minutes.

MRS. G.: But what was he *doing*?

MRS. GANTRY: Working out his weight, if you please.

MRS. G.: Not on the way down!

MRS. GANTRY: On the way down, Mabel. He'd left his diary, with his weight and everything in it, back at the caravan.

MRS. G.: Wouldn't it have done when he got home?

MRS. GANTRY: It was a question of knowing how hard to fall, Mabel. He needed to know his weight before he could work it out. (*Pause.*) And then after all that he found he'd fallen harder than he need have done. Made a mistake with one of the figures or something.

MRS. G.: It's easily done.

Pause.

MRS. GANTRY: Any other man would have known his weight, of course.

MRS. G.: You should make him carry his diary about with him, Myra.

Pause.

BARNES: (*off*). Where do you want this?

Light fades rapidly on living-room and comes up downstage Right where Barnes can be seen in his shirtsleeves. He has a panel in his hands and is facing off stage.

34

MR. G.: (*off*). What is it?

BARNES: Front panel. Top left.

MR. G.: (*off*). That goes over here. Give it to me.
*Mr. Groomkirby appears, takes the panel and
disappears.*

BARNES: We'd better start taking some of this round,
hadn't we? What about these side panels? Are
they ready to go?

MR. G.: (*off*). Yes. And the bolts. They can all go round.
We shall have to assemble them properly when
we've got them inside.

BARNES: Right. (*He begins to cross from Right to Left with a
large panel.*) Where do you want this? Outside the
kitchen window?

MR. G.: (*off*). That'll do.
*Stanley Honeyblock enters from Left and crosses
to Right.*

BARNES: (*over the top of the panel*). Hallo, Stan. I shouldn't
go that way round, if I were you.

STAN: Why? What's going on?

BARNES: Have a look. (*Going.*) Round the corner. Don't let
him see you, that's all. Unless you want to get
roped in. Noah's Ark isn't in it.

STAN: (*looking at disappearing panel*). What's that? A
coffin he's building himself?

BARNES: (*off*). He'll need one before he's finished, the way
he's going.
Stan shrugs and continues across.

STAN: (*over his shoulder to Barnes*). Haven't seen anything
of Sylvia, I suppose?

BARNES: (*off*). She's around somewhere, Stan.

STAN: (*going off*). Be another hour I expect before she's ready.
*Light comes up in living-room. Sylvia is going out
into the kitchen, having come in to fetch something.
She leaves the door open. Mrs. Groomkirby and
Mrs. Gantry are as before.*

MRS. G.: I wish I'd known sooner. I could have told Kirby.

MRS. GANTRY: Sooner?

35

MRS. G.: About Mr. Gridlake. He's always glad of an excuse to go into mourning.

MRS. GANTRY: Kirby likes his black, doesn't he?

MRS. G.: He's never out of it, Myra. That reminds me. Sylvia—if you're going upstairs in a minute you might just look in and see if Kirby's all right.

SYLVIA: (*off*). Why can't you stop fussing about him all the time, mum? He's perfectly all right.

MRS. G.: (*to Mrs. Gantry*). Knocked himself out up there.

MRS. GANTRY: Oh, dear.

MRS. G.: With his weights. He may want a ping if he's ready to come round. He does everything to the bell these days.

SYLVIA: (*off*). It'll do him good to lie there unconscious for a bit. Give his brain a rest.

MRS. G.: It wouldn't hurt you to look in and see, Sylvia.

SYLVIA: You know yourself what he's like, mum, if anybody interferes with him when he's unconscious. *Pause.*

MRS. G.: (*indicating the cash register*). That thing over there's been more trouble than it's worth ever since he came home with it.

MRS. GANTRY: I can't think why you don't have an ordinary bell rigged up for him, Mabel.

MRS. G.: No, he's got attached to that now. He bought it originally so he could have something to offer in part exchange if he ever wanted a typewriter—and now we seem to be stuck with it.

MRS. GANTRY: That must have been when he was working on his book.

MRS. G.: It was. When he was learning how to make the paper.

MRS. GANTRY: What happened about that, Mabel? Did he ever get any further with it?

MRS. G.: Oh, yes. He made enough paper to last us till kingdom come. Stacked up out there in bales— you can't move for it. *Pause.*

MRS. GANTRY: As long as he managed to get the book finished.

MRS. G.: He didn't seem to get much further with that, Myra. By the time he'd made the paper and got the ingredients together for his ink he'd lost the thread of his story.

Pause.

MRS. GANTRY: Pity. He could have written a nice book if he hadn't lost the thread.

Pause.

MRS. G.: (*with a nod towards the cash register*). So then of course it became an egg-timer—and now he uses it for everything practically. Every time he wants a ping.

Pause.

MRS. GANTRY: Rather novel.

MRS. G.: What?

MRS. GANTRY: Using it as an egg-timer.

MRS. G.: He won't trust his stop-watch. That's the real reason.

MRS. GANTRY: Oh?

MRS. G.: He's had it ever since he was ten, but he can't bring himself to trust it.

MRS. GANTRY: Fancy.

Pause.

MRS. G.: At least, he'll trust it for the minutes if he's in the mood, but . . .

MRS. GANTRY: . . . not for the seconds.

MRS. G.: He's afraid of being led up the garden.

MRS. GANTRY: I wonder why that is.

MRS. G.: I don't know, Myra, I'm sure. He's always been the same. (*Pause.*) Just the seconds.

Pause.

MRS. GANTRY: Perhaps he thinks he can check up better on the minutes and see that he's not being led up the garden.

MRS. G.: It may be that. He's certainly quite decided about it whatever it is. As far as the seconds are concerned.

Pause.

37

MRS. GANTRY: It's not so easy to keep check with the seconds. Unless you've got another stop-watch.

MRS. G.: He probably wouldn't trust that any more than he does his own, Myra.

MRS. GANTRY: They like to know where they are with things, don't they? Everything cut and dried and that. *Pause.*

MRS. G.: So of course there was nothing for it but to use the cash register and time his eggs with that. And the telephone, of course.

MRS. GANTRY: They're not worth eating unless they're done just right, are they?

MRS. G.: He won't touch them, Myra.
Sylvia enters from the kitchen and makes her way languidly and erratically to the door into the hall.

MRS. G.: Sylvia—what was the name of that man with the dogs Kirby always used to be on about?

SYLVIA: Oh—I keep *telling* you, mum, who he was.

MRS. G.: (*to Mrs. Gantry*). He used to ring a bell to make their mouths water.

SYLVIA: Pavlov.

MRS. G.: That's right. So of course next thing we knew he was giving himself a ping on the cash register every time he sat down to a meal. Now he can't do a thing without it.

MRS. GANTRY: Dependent on it.

MRS. G.: You know he wanted to *be* one of that man's dogs at one time?

SYLVIA: (*going out*). Oh—for goodness' sake, mum! (*She closes the door impatiently behind her.*)

MRS. G.: As a matter of fact I think that's what's at the bottom of half Kirby's trouble.

MRS. GANTRY: I must say I've never really visualized him as a dog, Mabel.

MRS. G.: He keeps on about being born too late and into the wrong species. I think it preys on him.

MRS. GANTRY: It's silly to hold it against himself.

MRS. G.: The same with his black. He won't wear his black

now unless he's got somebody to go into mourning
for.

MRS. GANTRY: Been killing people, I suppose?

MRS. G.: Not so far as I know, Myra. We don't say too
much about it to him because it only drives him
in on himself—but he thinks a lot too much about
death to be good for him.

MRS. GANTRY: Perhaps now he's got his music it might take his
mind off it a bit.

MRS. G.: Arthur's as bad really—although he's more taken
up with the legal side of it, of course. Books all
over the place. Look at them. They're all law
books of one kind or another. I've never finished
moving them about from one place to another.

MRS. GANTRY: They get very tied up in it, don't they?

MRS. G.: I spend half my time one way and another
between the two of them, tidying up and this,
that and the other.

MRS. GANTRY: I think they're all the same, Mabel.
Pause.

MRS. G.: What I'm dreading is the day he brings the Old
Bailey home for us all to fall over.

MRS. GANTRY: He's too wrapped up in his books, Mabel.

MRS. G.: I wouldn't be so sure, Myra. I've got a sort of
sixth sense about these things.
*Mr. Groomkirby appears downstage Right. He
crosses laboriously with a faint suggestion of sternly
repressed stealth from Right to Left in front of the
living-room set.*
*He is carrying the front end of a very long, very
high oak panel which completely masks the living-
room set as it passes across.*
*On the panel are the words 'THIS WAY UP'.
They are stencilled upside down at the bottom.*
*Mr. Groomkirby disappears off Left but the panel
continues to pass across. On it, as a kind of trade
mark, is the figure of Justice—blindfolded and with
sword and scales—also upside down. Above it,*

39

upside down, are the words: BUILD-IT-
YOURSELF. SERIES NINE—FAMOUS
INSTITUTIONS. NUMBER SEVEN: OLD
BAILEY.
When the other end of the panel comes into view
it is seen to be carried by Stan.
He looks less neat than he did, has obviously been
working hard, and looks very much like a forced
volunteer.
When the panel has passed across Mrs. Gantry is
preparing to go.

MRS. GANTRY: I think that's more or less everything, Mabel.
(*Rising.*) I haven't touched the gherkins, but I can
attend to those when I come in in the morning.

MRS. G.: Oh, don't worry about those, Myra. (*She goes to
the mantelpiece.*) It's the other things *I* can't
manage. You've no idea what a difference it makes
just having you come once or twice a week. What
did I do with your envelope?

MRS. GANTRY: And you want me first thing in the morning,
Mabel—is that right?

MRS. G.: If you could manage it, Myra.

AUNT M.: There's no alternative, Mabel. I shall have to go
by sedan chair.

MRS. G.: Here it is. (*Handing a small brown envelope to
Mrs. Gantry.*) That's for tonight and last Friday,
Myra. I think you'll find it's all there.

MRS. GANTRY: Last Friday?

MRS. G.: When you came in to give us a hand with the
leftovers.

MRS. GANTRY: (*putting the envelope just the same into her hand-
bag*). Oh, good heavens, Mabel—that was only a
few bits and pieces. You shouldn't have bothered.

MRS. G.: (*indicating Aunt Mildred*). I wondered when the
sedan chair was coming up. We always get that
when it's time for her to be going off to bed.

MRS. GANTRY: She'd be better off on a tricycle.

MRS. G.: (*moving towards the door*). It never seems to occur

40

to her that a sedan chair would be far too heavy
for her.

MRS. GANTRY: It needs two in any case.

MRS. G.: Of course it does.

MRS. GANTRY: One at the front and one at the back.

MRS. G.: She couldn't be in both places at once.

MRS. GANTRY: (*going*). *And* inside.

MRS. G.: And inside as well. (*Following Mrs. Gantry out.*)
It's too much for one person.
Mrs. Groomkirby closes the door behind her.
Light fades out on living-room.
*Stan appears downstage Right and is about to
cross to Left.*
*He has the air of someone who feels he is being
imposed on.*

STAN: She does know I'm here, I suppose?

MRS. G.: (*off*). What?

STAN: (*checking*). Sylvia. She's not waiting for me in
there or anything, is she?

MR. G.: (*off*). No. She'll be down when she's ready.
Stan continues across.

MR. G.: (*off*). It s in among the straw there somewhere.
Rolled up—with a rubber band round it. I can't
get on till I've got it. It'll be there if you look.
Marked 'blueprint'. In with the straw the brass
fittings were packed in.
Stan goes off.
Aunt Mildred is isolated in a strong light.

AUNT M.: If Maud Banquet were here now I could have
taken her out to look at the aurora borealis.
(*Pause.*) Or she could have stood on a chair and
seen it through the window in the station-master's
office. (*Pause.*) You can get a wonderful view
from the window in the station-master's office if
you stand on a chair. (*Pause.*) The last time I
took Maud Banquet to see the aurora borealis she
thought it was the signals. (*Pause.*) Look, Mildred,
she said. If it isn't those dreadful men in the

41

signal boxes—they've been carousing again!
Pause.

MRS. G.: (*opening door from hall and calling upstairs*). Are you up there for good, Sylvia? You'll have Stan here presently. *I'm* not entertaining him.

The opening of the door is the signal for the light to come up over the whole living-room.

As it does so, and while Mrs. Groomkirby is still at the door looking upstairs, Mr. Groomkirby is making his way out into the kitchen having apparently set up a witness box in the living-room. Mrs. Groomkirby closes the door, crosses briskly to Aunt Mildred, checks on seeing the witness box, looks at it for several seconds with incredulous hostility, turns away tight-lipped, and going up to Aunt Mildred unceremoniously takes her travel brochure and puts it back on its shelf on the other side of the room.

AUNT M.: Maud wanted to call it the northern lights, but I said No. (*Pause.*) Either we call it the aurora borealis, I said, or we don't call it anything at all. (*Pause.*) In the end we took it in turns.

Pause.

Mrs. Groomkirby has returned and is folding up Aunt Mildred's rug.

AUNT M.: Some days she'd call it the northern lights while I called it the aurora borealis. Some days it was the other way round.

Pause. Mrs. Groomkirby goes behind the wheelchair and begins to turn it in the direction of the kitchen door.

AUNT M.: She'd call it the aurora borealis while I called it the northern lights.

Pause. Mrs. Groomkirby wheels her briskly out past the witness box, which involves a slight detour.

AUNT M.: (*as she goes through the door*). We got on very well together.

Barnes appears downstage Left. He takes down his

42

*jacket from a peg just out of sight and moves just
to the edge of the set where he can see the witness
box. Having satisfied himself about this, he puts his
jacket over his arm and turns to the audience.*

BARNES: (*looking at his hands*). Go up and try and get some
of this off.
*He crosses to Right, pausing on the way for another
look at the witness box and to size up the room.*

BARNES: I hope he knows what he's doing, that's all.
Mrs. Groomkirby enters from hall.

MRS. G.: (*seeing Barnes*). Now what's he letting us all in
for? (*She indicates witness box.*)

BARNES: (*anxious to extricate himself as soon as possible*).
Hallo, Mrs. Groomkirby.

MRS. G.: What is it? A pulpit or something? Stuck right
where we can fall over it?

BARNES: (*edging off*). I think it's just a witness box.

MRS. G.: (*going to cupboard*). Doesn't he think I've got
enough to do moving his books from one place to
another?

BARNES: I shouldn't worry too much, Mrs. Groomkirby.

MRS. G.: (*going out to the kitchen*). It was bad enough when
he brought Stonehenge home and we had it stuck
in here for weeks.

BARNES: It probably won't come to anything.
*Barnes makes good his escape while he can with a
brief explanatory glance at the audience.
Mrs. Groomkirby addresses remarks from time to
time to Barnes, whom she thinks to be still within
earshot.*

MRS. G.: (*off*). Everybody calling us Druids behind our
backs. (*Pause.*) This time we shall have a lot of
jury men tramping all over the carpet every time
we want to sit down to a meal, as well. (*Longer
pause.*) What does he think we're going to do?
(*Glancing in at the witness box as she crosses past
the open door.*) Walk round *that* every time we
want to go from one side of the room to the

43

other? (*Pause.*) Next thing we know we shall have
the entire Old Bailey or something in here.
Collecting the dust. I wouldn't put anything past
him—once he gets an idea in his head. Before we
know where we are we shall be having walls
knocked out to make room for it and one thing
and another. (*Pause.*) (*Crossing back without
looking in.*) And the ceiling raised. (*Pause.*) (*Off.*)
Putting our hands in our pockets all the time for
chandeliers and cornices and goodness knows
what. (*Pause.*) And flunkeys. Under our feet.
(*Pause.*) A room the size he'll need for the Old
Bailey. We shan't know where we are. Upper
class, lower class, Tom, Dick or Harry or what.
We shall be on the phone half the time trying to
find out. (*Pause.*) What else has he got out there
to bring in? (*Pause.*) (*Appearing at the door.*) Is he
bringing anything else in?
*Mrs. Groomkirby looks around for Barnes, registers
his absence and turns to go out again.*
*The door from the hall opens and Sylvia enters. She
is wearing slightly more formal clothes and carries
an outdoor coat which she flings over a chair.*
*Mrs. Groomkirby glances round and continues
out.*

MRS. G.: I thought you'd gone, Sylvia.
*Sylvia holds her arms straight by her sides and
tries to see the effect in the mirror. This involves
standing on a chair.*

SYLVIA: How can I go out with my arms like this? Look
at them!
*Mrs. Groomkirby enters to put something away and
checks to glance at Sylvia's arms.*

MRS. G.: What's the matter with your arms?

SYLVIA: You can see what's the matter with them. You've
only got to look at them.
*Mrs. Groomkirby continues across the room and
then turns to go out.*

44

MRS. G.: You've been out with them like that often enough before. I can't see anything wrong with them.

SYLVIA: They're absolutely ridiculous!

MRS. G.: (*checking*). Turn round and let me see. Hold them naturally! They look just the same to me as they always do.

SYLVIA: That doesn't make them any better. (*Turning back to the mirror.*) Look where they reach to!

MRS. G.: (*making for the kitchen door*). I'm looking, Sylvia. They're perfectly all right. It's the proper length for them. Mine are exactly the same. So are your father's.

SYLVIA: (*getting impatiently down*). Oh for goodness' sake, mum!

Mrs. Groomkirby goes out into the kitchen.
Pause.

MRS. G.: (*off*). What time's Stan supposed to be coming?

SYLVIA: (*fuming*). Quarter of an hour ago!
Pause.

SYLVIA: (*Getting up again to look in the mirror*). If they started lower down it would be something.

MRS. G.: (*crossing past open door without looking in*). What difference would that make?
Pause.

SYLVIA: (*getting down and going to kitchen door*). Look where they reach to! Just look at that gap.

MRS. G.: (*appearing at door*). What gap?

SYLVIA: There!

MRS. G.: I don't know what you're talking about, Sylvia. I can't see any gap.
Sylvia gives up and goes across to the armchair.
Mrs. Groomkirby raises her eyes and goes off.
Sylvia throws herself moodily down in the chair.
Pause.

SYLVIA: If they didn't *start* so blessed high up I might be able to reach my knees with them!
Pause.

MRS. G.: (*off*). It's beyond me, Sylvia, why you should want to reach your knees with them!

Sylvia reacts impatiently but says nothing.

MRS. G.: (*off*). In any case you can bend down and do it, can't you?

SYLVIA: I don't *want* to have to bend down! That's the whole point!

Pause.

MRS. G.: (*off*). I suppose it's Stan we've got to thank for this.

SYLVIA: Oh—Stan, Stan, Stan! I wish you wouldn't keep on about *Stan* all the time! It's got nothing to do with Stan.

Pause.

MRS. G.: (*off*). In any case there isn't anything we can do about it now. (*Crossing past the open door without looking in.*) You should have thought of all this before you were born.

SYLVIA: For goodness' sake, mum! How *could* I have?

Mrs. Groomkirby enters and begins clearing away the remnants left by Mrs. Gantry.

MRS. G.: We're not turning you into some monstrosity or other just to satisfy one of your whims, Sylvia.

SYLVIA: (*scornfully*). Whim!

MRS. G.: (*going out to kitchen*). Making you look like an ape.

Mr. Groomkirby enters from the kitchen at the same time. He carries a toolbag.

Mrs. Groomkirby checks and watches him into the room.

Mr. Groomkirby goes to the witness box, sets down the toolbag, and taking out a screwdriver and screws, begins to screw down the witness box by means of metal brackets fixed to the bottom.

MRS. G.: That's a sensible place for a witness box, I must say.

Mr. Groomkirby remains silent in the manner of one who has moved on from words to action.

Mrs. Groomkirby goes out in eloquent silence.
Pause.

SYLVIA: At least apes can reach their knees without bending.

MRS. G.: (*reappearing and looking curiously at Sylvia*). Apes are bending all the time, Sylvia. (*After continuing to look at Sylvia for a moment, she goes off.*) As you well know.
Pause.

SYLVIA: Not all that much.
Pause.

MR. G.: (*without in any way diverting his attention from the job*). You'd need a complete new set of glands, Sylvia. We couldn't run to it.

MRS. G.: (*off*). She's spending too much time at the Zoo.
Pause.

SYLVIA: I don't know what it is you've both got against apes as far as that goes.

MRS. G.: (*off*). We've got nothing against apes, Sylvia. As such. (*Long pause.*) I thought we were leading up to something like this when you started on about your arms in the first place.

SYLVIA: (*starting up*). Oh!

MRS. G.: (*off*). It's only since you've been going to the Zoo with Stan two or three times a week that we've had all this.

SYLVIA: (*checking on her way to the door to the hall*). For the last time will you shut *up* about Stan, mum? For God's *sake*! It's got nothing to do with Stan! (*She makes for the door and opens it.*) Or the Zoo either as far as that goes. (*She goes out and closes the door behind her.*)

MRS. G.: (*off*). What with that and the Natural History Museum every weekend. I'm not surprised she gets hold of all these idiotic ideas. (*Pause.*) Spending all her time amongst a lot of mastodons and pterodactyls. (*Pause.*) (*Appearing at the door*

47

and addressing Mr. Groomkirby.) I blame Stan for all this, you know.

Mr. Groomkirby says nothing.

MRS. G.: (*indicating skull*). Look at that thing! Supposed to remind you of death. It's never worked since he gave it to her.

MR. G.: (*without looking up as Mrs. Groomkirby is about to go back into the kitchen*). You don't have to keep on at her all the time, Mabel.

Mrs. Groomkirby gives him a tightlipped look and goes back into the kitchen. She reappears with a tray and in silence goes to the table to clear the remains of the meal on to it.

MRS. G.: (*after a pause*). I notice you soon had something to say when you thought you might have to dip in your pocket for her for new glands.

Pause. Mrs. Groomkirby takes up the full tray and goes out with it.

(*as she goes through the door*). It won't last five minutes when she gets them. (*Pause*). (*Off*). Look at the mastodon. How long did that last?

Pause.

MR. G.: (*without looking up*). She might have made a go of the mastodon if you hadn't been on at her all the time, Mabel.

Mrs. Groomkirby appears with a tray on which a snack has been laid out.

MRS. G.: (*crossing with tray to door into hall*). In any case what man in his right senses is going to look twice at an ape?

Short pause.

MR. G.: Stan, for one.

MRS. G.: (*opening the door*). Stan!

At this moment Sylvia is entering by the same door. Simultaneously Stan comes in from the kitchen.

MRS. G.: (*going out and leaving Sylvia to close the door*). This is a fine time to be going out anywhere, I must say!

Instead of closing the door, Sylvia stands stockstill in dumbfounded horror. She is staring at Stan, who is framed in the kitchen doorway. He is dirty, dishevelled, and covered in straw.

STAN: Don't tell me you're ready, Sylvia. At last.

MR. G.: (*looking up*). Did you find it, Stan?

STAN: (*puzzled by Sylvia's scrutiny*). What's the matter? (*He moves to the mirror.*)

MR. G.: (*straightening up. Irritably.*) Wasn't it there?

SYLVIA: (*as Stan sees himself in the mirror*). What on earth do you think you look like?

MR. G.: He's been trying to find something, Sylvia. For me. (*Moving to the hall door.*) I think I know where I might have left it.

STAN: Lend me a clothes brush. (*Going out into the kitchen.*) Where do you keep it? Won't take a minute.
Pause. Sylvia is breathing heavily.

MR. G.: (*going out into hall*). It's all right, Stan. Don't worry. I'll find it.

STAN: (*off*). It's coming off. It's only a bit of straw.

SYLVIA: Is that *all*?

STAN: (*appearing with brush*). What do you mean? You don't imagine I *came* here like this, do you? (*Going.*) I thought I was doing someone a good turn.

SYLVIA: Not me, by any chance?

STAN: (*off*). If you'd been ready at the proper time I wouldn't have been let in for this in the first place. (*Appearing at the door more or less free from straw and with the brush in his hand.*) How's that? (*He is still dishevelled.*)

SYLVIA: Are you trying to make out it's *my* fault? *You've* got a nerve! Covered in a lot of old straw and muck!

STAN: If it's any interest to you, Sylvia, I've been helping your father.

SYLVIA: Oh, *have* you? (*Turning on her heel and going out.*)

49

Well, you'd better go and ask him if he's got any more jobs for you, hadn't you? (*She slams the door.*)

STAN: (*with an impulsive move towards the closing door*). Look, for God's sake, Sylvia! I can get home and change in ten minutes!

Stan turns away in furious frustration. The door immediately opens again. Stan wheels expectantly. Mr. Groomkirby enters, brandishing the rolled-up blueprint and leaving the door open.

MR. G.: Now perhaps we shall be able to see where we are.

Stan looks venomously at Mr. Groomkirby for a moment. Mr. Groomkirby spreads out the plan on the table and bends over it. Stan suddenly turns and vents his fury on the nearest object, which is the cash register. He brings his fist down and rings up No Sale. After the slightest of pauses a massed choir launches full-throatedly into the Hallelujah Chorus. Stan is momentarily electrified and then begins moving stealthily towards the door. Once at it he disappears with singleminded alacrity out into the hall. The front door is heard to shut.
Simultaneously the music is cut off and the set blacked out.
Stan appears downstage right crossing purposefully. Kirby appears on forestage. He appears dazed.

KIRBY: I might have been dreaming for all he knew!
Louder as Stan passes him without turning.
Might have stopped me stone dead in the middle of an orgasm!

STAN: (*going off*). Go to hell!
Fade out on Kirby.
Barnes, in an outdoor coat, comes on casually where Stan went off.

BARNES: That, I rather fancy, might be carrying coals to Newcastle—but never mind. (*Looking at his watch.*) Fifteen minutes? And then back here.

*Barnes continues across to go off Right, checks,
changes his mind and quickly goes off the way he
came as the houselights go up.*

END OF ACT ONE

ACT TWO

The living-room. Furniture has been crowded to
one side by the courtroom which dominates. Part
of one wall has had to go in order to make room
for it. Access to various parts of the room, and to
cupboards, involves squeezing with difficulty
round some part of the Court. Table, with two
chairs, is now downstage.
Even so, the Court is incomplete. There is a bench
for the Judge, a witness box to the Judge's left,
and benches for Counsel to his right.
Downstage Right is a small control panel for the
Court.
When the curtain rises MRS. GANTRY is seen sitting at
the table.
MRS. GROOMKIRBY has almost finished pressing a
pair of black trousers. The jacket is hanging on a
hanger nearby.

MRS. GANTRY: (rising as at exit in Act One). I think that's more
or less everything, Mabel.

MRS. G.: (switching off the iron and hanging up the trousers
on the hanger with the jacket). Finished, Myra?
I'll get your envelope.

MRS. GANTRY: I haven't touched the asparagus, but I can attend
to that first thing in the morning,

MRS. G.: (she leaves the suit hanging from a peg). Don't
worry about the asparagus, Myra. I can see to
that. It's those great packets of cereals they send
us. (She finds the envelope.) I think you'll find
that's right, Myra.

AUNT M.: (off). It's all the same, Mabel. Roller-skates,

roundabouts, rickshaws. As long as it's getting us
somewhere.

MRS. GANTRY: You've had to move her, then.

MRS. G.: (*indicating Court*). We can't get her in here for
this great white elephant. (*To Aunt Mildred.*)
You'd never be able to pull a rickshaw, Aunt
Mildred. (*To Mrs. Gantry as they go out together.*)
She wants something she can go over Niagara
Falls in.

MRS. GANTRY: (*at door*). She'd be better off with a barrel, Mabel.

MRS. G.: (*following Mrs. Gantry out and closing the door*). Of
course she would.
Short pause.
Sylvia enters from the hall in outdoor clothes.

SYLVIA: Come on. I thought you were supposed to be
ready.
*Stan appears from behind the control panel looking
at his watch.*

STAN: You know we were going to be there by quarter
to, don't you? It's now ten past.

SYLVIA: Well come on then.
*Stan makes a final adjustment to something behind
the panel and then switches it on as though to test it
briefly for sound.*

MRS. G.: (*entering as Sylvia is about to go out*). This is a
fine time to be going somewhere, I must say! (*She
catches sight of Stan in passing on her way to the
kitchen.*) The pair of you. (*She goes out.*)

SYLVIA: (*at door. Impatiently*). Oh come on, for goodness'
sake, and leave it.

JUDGE'S VOICE: . . . and even your own counsel has to admit that not
only were you as drunk as a wheelbarrow, but that
you were quite incapable of so much as falling flat
on your face when asked to do so. Moreover . . .

STAN: (*switching off and following Sylvia out*). I wonder
if he knows how much current this thing's going
to eat up. (*Calling.*) Good night, Mrs. Groomkirby. (*He goes out, closing the door behind him.*)

54

MRS. G.: (*entering with large tray*). Back goodness knows
       when, I suppose.
AUNT M: (*off*). Things seem to have been happening, Mabel.
       *Pause. Mrs. Groomkirby begins clearing everything
       from the table on to the tray.*
AUNT M.: They've put me where I can see through the
       window. (*Pause.*) I think I must be in the station-
       master's office, Mabel. (*Pause.*) I can see out
       through the window. (*Pause.*) Did you know there
       were two Red Setters at the end of the garden,
       Mabel? (*Pause.*) I can see them from where I'm
       sitting.
       *Pause. Mrs. Groomkirby takes up the full tray and
       moves downstage with it on her way to the kitchen
       as Mr. Groomkirby enters from the hall.*
       *He is wearing outdoor clothes and carries a large
       brown paper bag. He switches on the set from the
       control panel in passing, and puts the brown paper
       bag on a chair.*
MRS. G.: A Mr. Justice called. (*Going off.*) Something about
       being on circuit.
       *Mr. Groomkirby takes off his hat and coat, opens
       the bag, and takes out a Judge's robe and wig. He
       begins trying these on, but they are too large for him.*
MRS. G.: (*off*). To do with the mains, I expect. They've
       probably been looking at our electricity bills.
       (*Pause.*) What it's going to be like when it's *all*
       there eating up the current, goodness only knows!
       *The Judge materializes from out of the Court and
       advances upon Mr. Groomkirby who is at first
       unaware of him.*
AUNT M.: (*off*). Look at those two Red Setters, Mabel. I can
       see them from here at the end of the garden.
       (*Pause.*) They must be blue with cold out there,
       Mabel.
MRS. G.: (*off. Irritably*). Red Setters are *red*, Aunt Mildred!
       The Judge now confronts Mr. Groomkirby.
JUDGE: Your wig? Or mine, Mr. Groomkirby?

Mr. Groomkirby, overawed, removes the wig.

MR. G.: Oh. Perhaps I've got hold of the wrong one. I
thought . . .

JUDGE: It's an easy mistake to make, Mr. Groomkirby.

MR. G.: Yes—I'm sorry.
*Mr. Groomkirby removes the robe and puts it on
the Judge.*

MR. G.: Rather silly of me. (*He adjusts the robe and fetches
the wig.*) I thought it didn't seem quite right. (*He
puts the wig on the Judge.*)

JUDGE: (*as he turns to go*). You'll in all probability be
needed as a witness, Mr. Groomkirby. So be on
hand. It saves wasting the time of the Court.
*As the Judge disappears the Court begins gradually
to assemble. A policeman, in uniform but without
helmet, approaches Mr. Groomkirby with a sheet
of paper.*

POLICEMAN: Mr. Groomkirby?

MR. G.: Yes?

POLICEMAN: Through the door over there, please.
The Policeman looks round for someone else.

MR. G.: What's this for?

POLICEMAN: (*turning back to Mr. Groomkirby and jabbing with
his finger toward the kitchen door*). Out there. With
the other witnesses. (*Calling more respectfully.*)
Detective-Sergeant Barnes?
*Barnes appears downstage Left. Mr. Groomkirby
goes resentfully out into the kitchen.*

BARNES: Yes?

POLICEMAN: I think there's a strong possibility you may be
wanted, sir, a bit later on.

BARNES: Right. (*Looking round the room.*) Been letting
himself go a bit, hasn't he?

POLICEMAN: Beg your pardon, sir?

BARNES: (*with an offhand gesture towards the Court*). This
lot. Plenty of it for a living-room.

POLICEMAN: Don't know where to stop, do they, some of them.

BARNES: (*going to door*). In here?

56

POLICEMAN: That's right, sir.
Barnes and Policeman go off.
The Court is now assembled and awaiting the Judge.
The Clerk calls for the Court to rise. The Judge
enters, bows to the Court, sits. Prosecuting Counsel
rises.

PROS. COUN.: M'lord. (*Addressing Jury.*) The facts you have
heard so far in this case, members of the jury,
have been simple enough and I do not propose . . .

JUDGE: (*intervening*). I see no sign of the jury. Are they
here?

PROS. COUN.: I understand they are, m'lord.

USHER: (*intervening*). There is no jury box, m'lord. As yet.

JUDGE: And no jury either apparently.

USHER: They are here in spirit, m'lord.

JUDGE: I see. (*He ponders momentarily.*) As long as they
are here in one form or another. (*He nods to
Counsel.*)

PROS. COUN.: The facts to which I am now going to direct your
attention, members of the jury, and upon which it
will be necessary for you to exercise your judgment
in due course, concern the activities of the accused
on a day last summer when he was allegedly . . .

JUDGE: (*intervening*). Where is the accused? Is he in the
court?

PROS. COUN.: He is in the dock, m'lord.

JUDGE: (*looking at it*). I see no dock.

USHER: The dock has not yet arrived, m'lord.

JUDGE: Where is it?

USHER: I understand it is on its way, m'lord.
Pause.

JUDGE: With the accused in it.

USHER: Yes, m'lord.
Defending Counsel rises.

DEF. COUN.: There have been certain delays, m'lord.

JUDGE: Traffic lights, I suppose.

DEF. COUN.: That and other untoward occurrences, m'lord.

JUDGE: He should be here. I have already disorganized

57

my personal arrangements pretty considerably in order to accommodate the court by being present, and I do not propose to put myself to further inconvenience by having this case running over time. If the accused is not here, the hearing will have to go on without him.

DEF. COUN.: As your lordship pleases.

Defending Counsel sits. Prosecuting Counsel rises.

PROS. COUN.: The whereabouts of the accused, members of the jury, on that vital day when he was allegedly else-where, tally in every single particular with the whereabouts of the only other person who so far as we know was on the spot at the time, and who is in the court at this moment. The whereabouts of this other person are therefore of paramount importance, and I should like to call him to the witness box now. (*To Usher.*) Mr. Groomkirby, please.

The Usher goes off.

Mrs. Groomkirby appears from the kitchen carrying a hot water bottle. She crosses to the door into the hall.

MRS. G.: I'm going up, Arthur. (*She opens door.*) You might notice what time Sylvia gets back. (*She goes out and closes door.*)

The Usher returns, approaches the Clerk and whispers to him. The Clerk stands and turns to enter into a whispered discussion with the Judge while the Usher withdraws respectfully.

JUDGE: (*looking across to Usher and addressing him*). Is this an objection to swearing per se?

USHER: Only to swearing on the unexpurgated Bible, m'lord. I understand there are certain passages he takes exception to, m'lord. On moral grounds.

JUDGE: (*after a pause for reflection*). Is he prepared to swear on anything?

USHER: I understand he has no objection to swearing on 'Uncle Tom's Cabin', m'lord.

JUDGE: On what?

USHER: 'Uncle Tom's Cabin', m'lord.

JUDGE: (*to Clerk*). I thought the issue of slavery on the American plantations had been settled by Abraham Lincoln?

CLERK: (*looking for confirmation to Usher*). I gather he has been informed of this, m'lord.

USHER: Yes, m'lord.

JUDGE: What did he say?

USHER: He said 'Not in my world it isn't'. Those were his words, m'lord.

JUDGE: (*to Clerk*). Which world is he referring to?

CLERK: I understand he has one of his own, m'lord.

JUDGE: Then why isn't he in it?

CLERK: He says he was told to come here, m'lord.
Pause. The Judge considers.

JUDGE: If it's a genuinely conscientious objection, I suppose I shall have to allow it. Has he got this work with him in Court?

USHER: He has a copy, yes, m'lord.

JUDGE: Tell him to bring it to the witness box.
The Usher goes out behind the Court. Counsel for the Defence rises.

DEF. COUN.: With very great respect, m'lord.

JUDGE: Yes?

DEF. COUN.: I have discussed this with my learned friend, m'lord, and if your lordship has no objection I should be most obliged if your lordship would consider dispensing with the oath altogether in respect of this witness, m'lord. I understand that if the oath is administered there is a strong possibility of prevarication, m'lord.

JUDGE: You mean he's a liar?

DEF. COUN.: Only when on oath, m'lord. I am told he looks on the oath in the light of a challenge, m'lord.

JUDGE: That's entirely a matter for him. If he's lying I shall direct the jury accordingly.

DEF. COUN.: As your lordship pleases.
Prosecuting Counsel rises. Defending Counsel sits.

PROS. COUN.: Might I, m'lord, with your lordship's permission, suggest to my learned friend that evidence from this source be accepted by the defence in the spirit in which it is given?

JUDGE: I suppose there's no objection. It would certainly save the time of the Court.

Prosecuting Counsel sits. Defending Counsel rises.

DEF. COUN.: Thank you, m'lord. My learned friend has suggested a way out of the difficulty and this is entirely acceptable to the defence, m'lord.

The Judge nods briefly.

The Usher enters followed by Mr. Groomkirby, whom he directs into the witness box. Mr. Groomkirby takes the oath.

MR. G.: *(holding up a copy of 'Uncle Tom's Cabin').* I swear, by Harriet Beecher Stowe, that the evidence I shall give shall be the truth, the whole truth, and nothing but the truth.

JUDGE: You understand, do you, that you are now on oath?

MR. G.: I do, m'lord.

JUDGE: You understand what being on oath means?

MR. G.: Yes, m'lord.

JUDGE: It means that you have undertaken in the sight— in your case—of Harriet Beecher Stowe, to give honest answers, as honest and truthful as you can make them, in reply to questions which are shortly going to be put to you by learned counsel.

MR. G.: I understand that, m'lord.

JUDGE: Anything you are unsure about, or anything you have no direct knowledge of, you must not try to fill out in any way by the use of your imagination. You are here simply and solely to give the Court the facts as you know them. Anything more or less than this is not, and can never be, the truth. You must therefore in your answers avoid anything which is not to the best of your knowledge factually true. This is what the solemn undertaking you have given to the Court means.

MR. G.: I understand that, m'lord.

JUDGE: And you intend therefore to be bound by this undertaking?

MR. G.: No, m'lord.

JUDGE: You mean, in other words, that you intend to lie to the Court.

MR. G.: That is so, m'lord, yes.

JUDGE: A frank and honest reply.

Defending Counsel rises.

DEF. COUN.: With respect, m'lord.

JUDGE: Yes?

DEF. COUN.: This is a point for your lordship, but it would be of the greatest possible assistance to my friend and me, m'lord, and possibly to the jury later, if your lordship would give a ruling on this point of the witness's intended perjury at this stage, m'lord. The witness says he is lying, m'lord, but we have every reason to believe that in saying this he is lying.

JUDGE: And that he is, in fact, telling the truth?

DEF. COUN.: That is the dilemma we are in, m'lord.

JUDGE: No very great dilemma. This is clearly a witness of candid integrity upon whom it would be perfectly proper to place the utmost reliance.

DEF. COUN.: (*sitting*). As your lordship pleases.

Prosecuting Counsel rises.

PROS. COUN.: (*addressing Mr. Groomkirby*). Are you Arthur Rudge Groomkirby?

MR. G.: (*full of a confidence verging on truculence*). That's right, sir.

PROS. COUN.: And you live now—have been living since 1949—at 93 Chundragore Street.

MR. G.: Yes, sir. I had it done out back and front three years ago.

PROS. COUN.: By whom, Mr. Groomkirby?

MR. G.: By the deceased, sir.

JUDGE: (*intervening*). He was not, I take it, deceased at the time?

MR. G.: (*slightly patronizingly*). No, m'lord. He was alive when he did it.

PROS. COUN.: Mr. Groomkirby—I want you to cast your mind back a little way to the summer of last year. To the twenty-third of August. Do you happen to remember where you were, or what you were doing, on that day?

MR. G.: Yes, sir. I was in Chester-le-Street.

PROS. COUN.: What happened in Chester-le-Street on that day to cause you to remember it so clearly?

MR. G.: I interviewed someone there. About a life insurance.

PROS. COUN.: I take it you don't often go so far afield to interview people.

MR. G.: That's why I particularly remember it.

PROS. COUN.: I see. (*Pause.*) And this interview, you say, took place in Chester-le-Street on the twenty-third of August last year?

MR. G.: Yes, sir. It was a Tuesday.

PROS. COUN.: At what time on the Tuesday?

MR. G.: Three-fifteen, sir.

PROS. COUN.: At three-fifteen on Tuesday the twenty-third of August last year you were in Chester-le-Street interviewing this man about a life insurance policy.

JUDGE: (*testily*). He's already said he was.

PROS. COUN.: As your lordship pleases.

MR. G.: (*smugly*). It was a woman I interviewed. By the name of Myra Penelope Straightpiece Gantry.

PROS. COUN.: How certain are you, Mr. Groomkirby, of the exact time?

MR. G.: There was a clock striking the quarter just outside the window when I put my first question to her.

PROS. COUN.: And what was this first question, Mr. Groomkirby?

MR. G.: I asked her if there was anything she would like to add, sir.

JUDGE: (*intervening*). What was her reply?

MR. G.: It was in the form of a sentence, m'lord.

JUDGE: We know it must have been in the form of a sentence, but what form did the sentence take?

MR. G.: (*feeling in his pocket and bringing out a notebook*). I made a note of it at the time, m'lord. (*Reads from notebook.*) She said she had a string of pearls in the form of a necklace but she wore it round her waist for the tightness.

PROS. COUN.: She wore it round her waist for the tightness. Didn't this strike you as being a rather extraordinary remark for her to make?

MR. G.: I didn't take much notice of it at the time, sir.

PROS. COUN.: You didn't think it at all remarkable. But you made a note of it.

MR. G.: (*smugly*). I was interviewing her, sir.
Pause.
Mr. Groomkirby has passed from semi-truculence to a sort of cocky assurance, but this is from now on broken down, at first by imperceptible degrees and then more and more rapidly.

PROS. COUN.: Would you agree, Mr. Groomkirby, that there were at the time possibly several thousand other inhabitants of Chester-le-Street equally eligible for interview, by you or someone else, on the subject of life insurance?

MR. G.: I dare say there would have been, yes, sir.

PROS. COUN.: But out of several thousand eligible people, the one person to be interviewed that afternoon happened, by a curious coincidence no doubt, to have been this woman, Myra Gantry?

MR. G.: If you put it like that, yes, I suppose that would be true.

PROS. COUN.: Even though the chances against it were several thousand to one?

MR. G.: I hadn't really thought of it in the light of a coincidence.

PROS. COUN.: Would you also agree, Mr. Groomkirby, that—confining ourselves to these islands alone—some-

MR. G.: thing of the order of fifty million people could, if the need had arisen, have gone to Chester-le-Street and interviewed this woman that afternoon?

MR. G.: I should think probably something of that order, yes, sir.

PROS. COUN.: The chances, in fact, were almost fifty million to one against its being you who did so?

MR. G.: I remember doing so, sir. I made a note of it at the time.

PROS. COUN.: Very well. And the time of this interview was three fifteen. A clock, you told us, was striking outside.

MR. G.: That's right, sir. I could hear it from where I was standing.

PROS. COUN.: And precisely at that very moment, when not one but both hands of the clock were at virtually the same point on the dial—at the figure three—precisely at the moment when the clock was striking the quarter, you put your first question to Myra Gantry.

MR. G.: (defiantly). Yes, sir.

PROS. COUN.: Perhaps you hadn't thought of that as a coincidence either, Mr. Groomkirby?

MR. G.: That was what happened, sir.

PROS. COUN.: You see, Mr. Groomkirby, this statement seems to be based upon a whole chain of these—to say the least of it—extraordinary coincidences. This question you put to Myra Gantry. You say it was your first. But in the course of an interview of this kind you might well have put twenty or thirty questions to her. This one, which happened—so we are asked to believe—to have been the first, could equally well it seems to me have been the seventh or the third or the twenty-ninth.

MR. G.: No, sir. It was the first.

PROS. COUN.: And this answer she is supposed to have given you. Goodness knows the words alone in the English language must be enough in all their

64

various forms virtually to defy computation—the possible ways of combining them must be infinite. And yet it was precisely *this* combination she hit on.

MR. G.: I made a note of it, sir.

PROS. COUN.: I know you did, Mr. Groomkirby. She said I have a string of pearls in the form of a necklace but I wear it round my waist for the tightness.

JUDGE: (*intervening*). For the what?

PROS. COUN.: For the tightness, m'lord.

MR. G.: That's what she said, sir.

Pause. Prosecuting Counsel sighs.

PROS. COUN.: Coincidence after coincidence. (*Lazily flicking through his papers.*) For instance you say all this took place on a Tuesday.

MR. G.: Tuesday the twenty-third of August, sir.

PROS. COUN.: You see, Mr. Groomkirby, I have here a calendar for last year and for a number of years prior to that. And I find that since 1950 there has been only one year in which the twenty-third of August has fallen on a Tuesday.

MR. G.: It fell on a Tuesday last year, sir.

PROS. COUN.: (*lazily delivering the coup de grâce*). The very year, in fact, when it so happened that Tuesday the twenty-third of August was the day you were in Chester-le-Street interviewing Myra Gantry.

MR. G.: (*dogged now, rather than cocky*). That's where I was, sir.

Long pause. Prosecuting Counsel flicks through his papers preparatory to changing course.

PROS. COUN.: (*in a quiet, bored voice*). There must have been quite a number of places from which you absented yourself on that rather vital twenty-third of August, Mr. Groomkirby, in order to be in Chester-le-Street?

MR. G.: I dare say that would be so, yes, sir.

PROS. COUN.: You were not, for instance, in London?

MR. G.: No, sir.

PROS. COUN.: Or Paris?

MR. G.: No, sir.

PROS. COUN.: Or Rome?

MR. G.: No, I wasn't there, sir.

PROS. COUN.: You were not, I imagine, in Reykjavik either?

MR. G.: I couldn't say for sure where that is, sir.

PROS. COUN.: Yet you absented yourself from it?

MR. G.: As far as I know, I did, yes.

PROS. COUN.: *And* from Kostroma.

MR. G.: I suppose I must have done.

PROS. COUN.: And Chengtu, and Farafangana, and Pocatello.

MR. G.: I'm afraid I'm not all that much good at geography.

PROS. COUN.: Not much good at geography, Mr. Groomkirby, yet you want the Court to believe that in order to be present at Chester-le-Street you absented your-self from a whole host of places which only an expert geographer could possibly be expected to have heard of.

MR. G.: (*beginning to flag*). That's where I thought I was, sir.
Pause.

PROS. COUN.: (*changing course again*). It is a good many months since all this happened, is it not, Mr. Groom-kirby?

MR. G.: Several months, yes, sir.

PROS. COUN.: You have no doubt in your mind, all the same, that this person who interviewed Myra Gantry last August was the person I am addressing now?

MR. G.: It was me, sir.

PROS. COUN.: It was you. (*Pause.*) Mr. Groomkirby—do you know what happens to the body in sleep?

MR. G.: It recuperates its energies, sir.

PROS. COUN.: Certain chemical and other changes take place, do they not?

MR. G.: I understand they sometimes do, yes, sir.

PROS. COUN.: You must have spent a good many hours in sleep since last August?

MR. G.: I dare say that would be true, sir.

The Judge begins to look at Mr. Groomkirby with suspicion and curiosity from time to time.

PROS. COUN.: You must have eaten a good many meals, and absorbed a fair amount of food?

MR. G.: Yes, sir.

PROS. COUN.: It would be true to say, would it not, that the normal processes of what is known sometimes as metabolism, whereby body tissue is constantly being built up or broken down, have been going on unceasingly since the twenty-third of August last year?

MR. G.: I couldn't say, sir.

The Judge looks up and continues to stare intently at Mr. Groomkirby with the same curiosity and suspicion as before.

PROS. COUN.: I suggest to you, Mr. Groomkirby, that in view of these changes the man you say was in Chester-le-Street last year is not the man who is standing in the witness box at this moment.

JUDGE: (*intervening*). Are you suggesting he's someone else?

PROS. COUN.: It is the contention of the prosecution, m'lord, that he has been gradually replaced in the inter-vening period by the man who is now before the court.

JUDGE: (*to Mr. Groomkirby, accusingly*). Is this so?

MR. G.: It's difficult to say, sir.

JUDGE: Do you mean you're not *sure*?

MR. G.: Not to say sure, no, m'lord.

The Judge looks intently at Mr. Groomkirby for a moment longer and then nods to Counsel.

PROS. COUN.: Where were you, Mr. Groomkirby, before you came here today?

MR. G.: I was living in a world of my own, sir.

PROS. COUN.: Where, roughly, would this world be in relation to, say, Chester-le-Street?

MR. G.: Quite some way away.

67

PROS. COUN.: Your presence there, in other words, entailed travelling some distance.

MR. G.: Quite some distance, yes.

PROS. COUN.: Do you enjoy travelling, Mr. Groomkirby?

MR. G.: On the contrary, sir.

JUDGE: (*intervening*). You mean you actively dislike it?

MR. G.: Actively dislike it, m'lord.

PROS. COUN.: You actively dislike travelling and yet you made this lengthy journey to Chester-le-Street?

Mr. Groomkirby's answers are beginning to be made wildly at random in an attempt to satisfy the Court and so escape from it.

MR. G.: I was a masochist at the time, sir.

JUDGE: (*intervening*). A what?

PROS. COUN.: A masochist, m'lord. A term employed in certain quarters to denote an addiction to pain as a source of pleasure.

JUDGE: (*to Mr. Groomkirby*). Where does the pain come into it?

MR. G.: (*wildly*). I had myself tattooed on the way, m'lord.

JUDGE: Where?

MR. G.: On the train, m'lord, between Boreham Wood and . . .

JUDGE: Whereabouts on the body?

MR. G.: I had one done on my left arm, m'lord, and a Crown and Anchor on my right hip as we came into Watford.

JUDGE: Were there any others?

MR. G.: There was a butterfly design between my shoulder blades, m'lord.

JUDGE: Was this put on after the others?

MR. G.: Before, m'lord.

The Judge intensifies his look of suspicion.

MR. G.: In a tunnel outside Leeds.

JUDGE: How was it done?

MR. G.: (*relaxing momentarily on what seems safe ground*). It was done with a needle, m'lord.

JUDGE: We know it must have been done with a needle, but how well was it done?

MR. G.: (*nonplussed again*). Do you mean in my own opinion, m'lord?

JUDGE: In anyone's opinion!

MR. G.: I think it was up to standard, m'lord.

The Judge continues to stare for a moment at Mr. Groomkirby and then with the air of a man whose mind is made up nods to Counsel.

PROS. COUN.: You say you were a masochist, Mr. Groomkirby. Are you a masochist now?

MR. G.: (*fervently*). No, sir.

PROS. COUN.: When did you cease your masochism?

MR. G.: A month or two ago, sir.

PROS. COUN.: And what made you give it up?

MR. G.: It was taking up too much of my time.

JUDGE: (*intervening*). Too much of your time? And how long had you been a masochist when you suddenly decided that your time was so valuable that you could no longer spare any of it for your masochism?

MR. G.: For something like three or four years, m'lord.

PROS. COUN.: What was it that made you take it up in the first place?

MR. G.: I was at a loose end at the time, sir.

The Judge looks sharply up.

PROS. COUN.: You were at a loose end. Would you tell the court, Mr. Groomkirby, as clearly as you can in your own words, exactly how loose this end was?

MR. G.: It was worn right down, sir.

JUDGE: (*intervening*). Worn right down. That tells us very little. Was it swinging loose? Was it rattling about?

Counsel, with a barely perceptible sigh and the briefest of glances towards Counsel for the Defence, sits down.

MR. G.: It was practically hanging off, m'lord.

JUDGE: And this is the end you say you were *at*? This

	loose end that in your own words was practically hanging off?
MR. G.:	I was pretty nearly at it, m'lord.
JUDGE:	You told the Court a moment ago you were at it. Now you say 'pretty nearly at it'. Which of these assertions is the true one?
MR. G.:	It was touch and go, sir.
JUDGE:	What was?
MR. G.:	Whether I fell off, sir.
JUDGE:	And what prevented you?
MR. G.:	It was that or take up masochism, m'lord.
JUDGE:	I see. The facts are beginning to emerge. You took up masochism when you began to realize that unless you did so the end you were at might come away and you with it. And you remained loyal to your masochism just so long as it suited you.
PROS. COUN.:	(*rising*). With very great respect, m'lord . . .
JUDGE:	The moment it was no longer useful to you you abandoned it without the slightest compunction. I can find no possible shred of excuse for behaviour of this kind.
DEF. COUN.:	. . . if I might have your indulgence for a moment, m'lord . . .
JUDGE:	The law would be moribund if it were unable to deal with a case such as this, and I should be failing in my duty if I were to allow a man of the kind you have shown yourself to be to go at large.
PROS. COUN.:	The *accused* will be here at any moment, m'lord. *Pause. Prosecuting Counsel sits in despair.*
JUDGE:	You will be remanded in custody while arrangements are being made to have you sent back to the world you have come from and claim to have been living in, where your activities will be of no concern to anyone but yourself. *Fast fade out lingering for a moment on the Judge. Pause.* *Door into hall opens. The light outside in the hall shows Mrs. Groomkirby in a dressing-gown, standing*

70

at the door she has half opened fumbling with the switch and then speaking into the darkened room.

MRS. G.: *Now* what have you done? Fused the lights, I suppose?

There is no reply. She puts her head round the door but, seeing nothing, withdraws it again.

MRS. G.: If you're going to stay down here waiting up for the dawn again, I'll put this light out.

Mrs. Groomkirby waits for a reply. None comes.

MRS. G.: (*Closing door*). And then for goodness' sake come up to bed.

Pause.

The Judge and Mr. Groomkirby become dimly visible downstage.

JUDGE: Well, Mr. Groomkirby. There's rather more here than meets the eye, don't you think?

Pause.

MR. G.: (*there is a defensive edge on his voice*). They've got the blinds down.

JUDGE: Possibly. (*Pause.*) At all events we shall know as soon as it's light enough to see anything.

Pause.

MR. G.: (*there is a surly edge on his defensiveness*). We're not going to see much with the blinds down.

Mr. Groomkirby becomes cowed, sullen, resentful, belligerent by turns.

JUDGE: You should have brought a torch, Mr. Groom-kirby.

Pause.

The Judge approaches the table, which is now downstage and has a chair on either side of it.

JUDGE: (*about to sit at the table where he can see Mr. Groomkirby*). In the meantime (*sitting*) perhaps it would be best if we were to play three-handed whist together.

MR. G.: Just the two of us?

Pause.

JUDGE: How many did you want, Mr. Groomkirby?

71

Mr. Groomkirby finds himself moving imperceptibly
nearer to the Judge.

MR. G.: Three-handed whist isn't a game to play between
two people.

JUDGE: I see. And why not, Mr. Groomkirby?
Pause.

MR. G.: (*moving still nearer*). And even if it were, we can't
see to play.

JUDGE: Only because there isn't enough light, Mr. Groomkirby. Where are the cards?

MR. G.: I haven't got any cards.

JUDGE: You mean you've lost them?

MR. G.: I never had any.
Pause.

JUDGE: I think it might be as well, Mr. Groomkirby, if
you were to go outside and look for some light.
Mr. Groomkirby is seen to hesitate for a moment.
Then his resistance crumbles and he moves off.
Pause.
Mr. Groomkirby returns.
Pause.

JUDGE: Well?

MR. G.: Not a sound.
Pause.

JUDGE: Oh. (*Pause.*) And the light?
Pause.

JUDGE: What about the light?

MR. G.: I didn't see any.

JUDGE: Where did you look?

MR. G.: I had my eyes shut. (*Pause.*) I don't intend to be
blinded suddenly by the sunrise.
Pause.

JUDGE: Or deafened, I suppose—by the dawn chorus.
(*Pause.*) What precautions are you taking against
that?
Pause.

MR. G.: (*reluctantly*). I wear earplugs.
Pause.

72

JUDGE: That perhaps is why you weren't able to hear anything out there, Mr. Groomkirby.

MR. G.: There was nothing to hear!

Pause.

JUDGE: You were wearing earplugs, Mr. Groomkirby.

MR. G.: It was silent out there, I tell you!

JUDGE: Faulty earplugs evidently.

Pause.

JUDGE: You could be as sure as you like about it as long as you knew your earplugs to be faulty.

Pause.

JUDGE: But not otherwise, Mr. Groomkirby.

Pause.

JUDGE: *Were* they faulty?

Pause.

JUDGE: I'm asking you a question! Were your earplugs faulty?

MR. G.: What if they were?

JUDGE: I see.

Pause.

MR. G.: What is it to you if I wear faulty earplugs?

Pause.

JUDGE: We'll play three-handed whist, shall we?

The Judge begins shuffling imaginary cards and then deals them on to the table.

MR. G.: (*slowly drawing nearer to the table*). Who's going to be dummy?

JUDGE: You, Mr. Groomkirby.

Pause.

MR. G.: (*sitting*). I've got my own hand to play.

JUDGE: You can leave that to me.

Pause.

MR. G.: (*picking up his cards*). It's too dark for this sort of thing.

Both go through the motions of playing whist.

MR. G.: If you play my hand, who's going to play yours?

JUDGE: I don't think we need either of us worry too much about that.

73

Pause. They continue to play in silence.

JUDGE: It's in some ways a pity you forgot to bring the cards, Mr. Groomkirby, but we seem to be managing quite well without them. My trick.
Pause. The game continues.

MR. G.: I feel cold.

JUDGE: You should have taken precautions.
Pause. The game continues.

JUDGE: My trick.

MR. G.: What possible precautions could I have taken?

JUDGE: You could have come here for one thing on a warmer night.

MR. G.: There aren't any warmer nights at this time of the year.

JUDGE: My trick.

MR. G.: You know that as well as I do.

JUDGE: (*gathering up the cards*). Go and see whether it's light yet outside. There's a good fellow.
Mr. Groomkirby hesitates, then gets up and goes out as before. He returns and sits down. Pause.

JUDGE: Well?

MR. G.: Frost.
Pause.

JUDGE: You were right then about its being cold, Mr. Groomkirby.

MR. G.: It's colder in here than it was outside.

JUDGE: You may well be right about that too, Mr. Groomkirby. But is it darker?
Pause.

JUDGE: I said is it darker in here than it was outside?

MR. G.: How the hell can I tell? You know I'm as blind as a bat with my eyes closed!
Pause.

JUDGE: Mr. Groomkirby. I wonder if you'd mind taking out your earplugs for a moment.
Mr. Groomkirby reluctantly takes them out.

JUDGE: Well?
Pause.

JUDGE: What do you notice?

Mr. Groomkirby makes signs with his hands.

JUDGE: Do you notice anything?

Mr. Groomkirby begins again making signs and then with a shrug abandons the attempt.

JUDGE: What's the matter with you?

Mr. Groomkirby sits motionless.

JUDGE: Cold, blind, deaf—and now dumb! (*Loudly.*) For God's sake, Mr. Groomkirby! Put your earplugs back in!

Mr. Groomkirby begins slowly replacing his earplugs.

JUDGE: Why do I shout? I dare say he can't hear a word without his crutches.

MR. G.: You think I'm paralysed, don't you?

JUDGE: I don't doubt you'll show us a clean enough pair of heels once your teeth have had proper attention.

Pause.

JUDGE: (*savagely*). Are you dentally fit?

Pause.

JUDGE: No. I thought not.

The lights come fully up. The courtroom is empty but for the three weighing machines of ACT ONE which stand, covered up, in the well of the Court.

MR. G.: (*with monumental relief*). Dawn!

JUDGE: (*rising*). Punctual as ever!

At the kitchen door is Sylvia. She is in her stockinged feet and carrying her shoes in her hand. The other hand is on the light switch as the lights go up, but she takes it away in order to signal to someone else out of sight in the kitchen. She retreats and closes the door.

The Judge looks at his watch as he rises, and then from his watch across to the death's head on the mantelpiece as though at a clock and compares the 'time'. He then goes up to the death's head, takes it up and shakes it as though starting a clock which has stopped. He puts it to his ear and, satisfied, replaces it.

He turns away and without a glance at Mr. Groom-
kirby goes into the courtroom and out of sight.
Mr. Groomkirby has the air of a man coming round
after a concussion. He has got up and made his way
in a dazed manner towards the courtroom.

MR. G.: God! What a night!

He goes, still dazed, to the Clerk's table, where he
absentmindedly gathers up some papers and wanders
off out of sight with them.
Sylvia tentatively opens the kitchen door.

SYLVIA: (*looking in. Good-humouredly.*) Don't be a fool,
Stan. He didn't say any such thing!

STAN: (*off*). Ask Tony. He was there.

SYLVIA: (*entering*). Come on. It's all clear.

STAN: (*off*). Right. Do you know there's some food out
here on a tray? And a flask?

SYLVIA: (*pirouetting round the room*). Bring it in then. (*As
Stan enters with tray.*) I don't believe he said any
such thing. What did *she* say?

STAN: (*putting the tray down*). I don't know. I didn't
stop to listen.

SYLVIA: We could do with some music.

STAN: There probably is some if you open the door.
(*Mimicking.*) Doh me soh doh soh.

They both take this up as a sort of comic duet, and
then, hotting it up, begin to jive to it.

STAN: (*as they approach the cash register*). Let's get the
Hallelujah Chorus. (*He clouts the cash register in*
passing.)

SYLVIA: (*breaking from him*). Don't be such a fool, Stan!
You'll have mum down here!

Stan goes to the door into the hall and opens it.

STAN: (*listening in mock consternation*). Not a sound.

Sylvia has crossed to the tray.

SYLVIA: You didn't bring any mustard in.

STAN: (*with exaggerated mock gallantry*). Good God!
(*Going posthaste into kitchen.*) How *could* I have
been so very careless!

76

Sylvia turns and looks into the mirror.

STAN: (*off*). Where the devil is it, anyway?

Sylvia has caught sight in the mirror of something behind her and transfixed with horror does not reply. Instead she spins round and faces the mantelpiece, gives a terrified look in the direction of her skull, and then turning away buries her face in her hands.

STAN: (*off*). It's all dried up, the only bit I can find out here. You'll have to do without by the look of it.

Sylvia has drawn her hands down her face and is looking out front with an expression of bewildered hopelessness.

Stan enters, sees Sylvia, and checks.

STAN: (*with a kind of dumbfounded solicitude*). What's the matter, Sylvia?

Sylvia looks straight ahead.

SYLVIA: (*flat voice*). Someone's been messing about with my death's head.

Stan looks across at the skull and back to Sylvia.

SYLVIA: (*turning and going out*). It wasn't working when you gave it to me.

Stan takes a step towards her, stops, watches her out of the room, and then turns to look at the skull. He stares at it for a time, then gazes down at the floor several feet in front of him and begins to turn away towards the kitchen door behind him.

On an impulse, and mastering a strong reluctance, he goes instead up to the mantelpiece, takes up the skull, puts it straight into his pocket and turning on his heel goes out through the kitchen.

Pause.

Mr. Groomkirby emerges from the courtroom in a manner suggesting that he has been wandering around behind it all the time in a kind of trance, and with every sign of exhaustion makes his way slowly to the door into the hall.

When he reaches it he switches off the light in the room, which is now in total darkness.
As though at a signal the sound of Doh me soh doh soh comes from upstairs.
By the light in the hall Mr. Groomkirby can be seen to check, stiffen, listen, and then quite suddenly on an angry impulse turn back into the room, slam the door and so cut off the sound, and with a stride to the control panel violently switch on the Court.

MRS. G.: *(appearing at door).* What's going on, Arthur?
The Court is assembled.

USHER: Silence.
Prosecuting Counsel is on his feet addressing the Judge.

PROS. COUN.: The accused is Kirby Groomkirby.

MRS. G.: *(crossing to pick up suit).* Oh, he'll need his suit then.
Mrs. Groomkirby crosses back with suit and goes out, taking Mr. Groomkirby with her.
Come on up, Arthur.

PROS. COUN.: M'lord, the facts, as your lordship is aware, are not in dispute in this case. The accused, Kirby Groomkirby, has admitted in the Magistrate's Court that between the first of August last year and the ninth of April he has been fairly regularly taking life, and since the case was heard there three weeks ago has asked for nine other offences in addition to the thirty-four in the original indictment to be taken into account, making a total altogether of forty-three. On the last occasion on which he took a life he was warned by Detective-Sergeant Barnes that complaints had been lodged and that action would be taken against him if he failed to conform to the law. It was after this, while he was preparing to repeat the offence, that Detective-Sergeant Barnes arrested him.

JUDGE: This would have been the forty-fourth offence?

PROS. COUN.: Yes, m'lord, but it was never carried out.

JUDGE: Because he was arrested.

PROS. COUN.: Yes, m'lord.

JUDGE: (*with heavy sarcasm*). It would be a pity to credit him with the wrong number of offences.

PROS. COUN.: He went before the Magistrate's Court on the third of this month where he pleaded guilty and was remanded for sentence. Since then he has asked for the nine other offences to be taken into account.

JUDGE: Are these nine offences exactly similar?

PROS. COUN.: They are exactly the same, m'lord, except that the victims are different.

JUDGE: Naturally the victims wouldn't be the same. What method has he been using?

PROS. COUN.: He seems to have been using the same technique fairly consistently, m'lord. He tells his victim a joke, waits for him to laugh, and then strikes him with an iron bar.

JUDGE: (*after pondering for a second*). Is there any previous record?

PROS. COUN.: No, m'lord.

JUDGE: He's been in no other kind of trouble at all?

PROS. COUN.: None at all, m'lord.

JUDGE: I see.

The Judge writes. Prosecuting Counsel sits.

JUDGE: (*to Defending Counsel*). Yes?

DEF. COUN.: (*rising*). M'lord, I should like to begin by calling Detective-Sergeant Barnes to the witness box. *Barnes is shown into the witness box by the Usher and sworn.*

BARNES: I swear by Almighty God that the evidence I shall give shall be the truth, the whole truth, and nothing but the truth. Detective-Sergeant Barnes, Gamma Division.

DEF. COUN.: Sergeant Barnes, you I believe spoke to the accused and to his parents, shortly before he was arrested?

BARNES: That is so, yes, sir.

79

DEF. COUN.: Would it be true to say that you found him very communicative and helpful?

BARNES: He was as communicative as I understand he usually is, yes, sir.

DEF. COUN.: And helpful?

BARNES: He was quite helpful, yes, sir.

DEF. COUN.: Whom did you see first, Sergeant Barnes—the accused or his parents?

BARNES: I saw his parents to begin with, sir

DEF. COUN.: What did you say to them?

BARNES: I put the position to them, sir, and told them that complaints had been received about their son's conduct . . .

DEF. COUN.: Yes—I'm sorry to interrupt you, Sergeant Barnes, but perhaps you can tell the court what in so many words you said on this first occasion?

BARNES: Yes, I think I can remember what I said, sir. When I went in, the first person I saw was Mr. Groomkirby, so I addressed what I had to say to him. I said, to the best of my recollection, something to the effect that 'It's beginning to add up down at the mortuary, Mr. Groomkirby'.

JUDGE: (*intervening*). Meaning that you were keeping a check of this man's victims?

BARNES: We were rather pressed for space, m'lord.

JUDGE: I know that, Sergeant. What I'm asking you now is whether your remark 'It's beginning to add up down at the mortuary' referred to this man's victims only, or to those of other people as well.

BARNES: It was a kind of joke, m'lord. I was trying to keep on friendly terms at that stage and I made the remark in a somewhat humorous manner. I went on to say 'We haven't got the Albert Hall, Mr. Groomkirby'.

JUDGE: So you weren't giving information?

BARNES: Not what you might call information, no, m'lord. *The Judge returns the ball to Counsel.*

DEF. COUN.: What did Mr. Groomkirby say to you, as far as

you can remember, Sergeant Barnes, in reply to that remark of yours?

BARNES: It was Mrs. Groomkirby, sir. She said 'We shall have to have another word with him, Arthur'.

JUDGE: (*intervening*). Who is Arthur?

DEF. COUN.: The father, m'lord.

JUDGE: Arthur Groomkirby.

DEF. COUN.: Yes, m'lord. (*To Barnes.*) Did you get the impression from the conversation you had with the mother and father of the accused, Sergeant Barnes, that they were doing all they could to help their son and take his mind off law-breaking?

BARNES: I got the impression that they were very concerned at the turn things seemed to have been taking, sir.

DEF. COUN.: And genuinely determined to do what they could for their son, to get him to mend his ways?

BARNES: Yes, sir.

DEF. COUN.: And the accused—it would be true to say, wouldn't it, Sergeant Barnes, that he rather confided in you?

BARNES: He told me certain things about himself, yes, sir.

DEF. COUN.: Can you tell his lordship what you were able to gather from this conversation with the accused—and his parents—about his character in general, and what you think may have caused him to act as he did?

BARNES: He seemed to have a strong desire, m'lord, to wear black clothes. He told me he'd had it for as long as he could remember, and his mother, m'lord, told me the same. For the last year or two he's been studying what he calls logical analysis, and this has gradually taken the form of looking for a logical pretext for wearing his black clothes. Prior to that I understand he just wore them without concerning himself about finding a pretext, m'lord.

JUDGE: There's nothing reprehensible in his wanting to be rational about it.

BARNES: No, m'lord. But with the accused it seems to have combined rather adversely with this urge to wear black, m'lord.

JUDGE: In what way?

BARNES: He said he had to have rational grounds for wearing it, m'lord.

JUDGE: Yes?

BARNES: And he hit upon this idea of going into mourning.

JUDGE: For his own victims, I suppose.

BARNES: For his own victims, m'lord.

JUDGE: (*after pondering for a second*). Surely there must have been plenty of people dying from natural causes.

BARNES: He wouldn't wear mourning for anyone he didn't know, m'lord. I put that specifically to him. He said he felt it would be a mockery, m'lord.

JUDGE: Was he sincere about this?

BARNES: I think he was, m'lord, yes.

Judge nods imperceptibly to Counsel.

DEF. COUN.: I want you to look now, Sergeant, at the weighing machines there in front of the witness box. (*To Usher.*) Could we have Exhibit Nine uncovered, please.

The covers are removed from the weighing machines.

DEF. COUN.: Have you seen these machines, or machines like them, Sergeant, before?

BARNES: Yes, sir. I have.

DEF. COUN.: Where did you see them?

BARNES: They were upstairs with a good many more, sir, at the house where I interviewed the accused, sir.

DEF. COUN.: Are these the ordinary kind of weighing machines such as anyone going into an amusement arcade or into a chemist's shop might expect to find?

BARNES: They are a fairly common type, yes, sir.

DEF. COUN.: They are, in fact, what are sometimes known as Speak-your-weight machines?

BARNES: Yes, sir.

DEF. COUN.: How many of these machines did you find when you went to the house at which the accused was living?

BARNES: A good many, sir. I didn't count them, but I should say running into several hundred.

DEF. COUN.: Would the number you saw be consistent with there being five hundred of these machines?

BARNES: It would be consistent with that, yes, sir.

DEF. COUN.: Were you able to discover in your conversation with the accused, Sergeant Barnes, any motive he might possibly have for building up this exceptionally large collection of Speak-your-weight machines?

BARNES: He did refer to them, sir. I didn't set much store by what he said because I thought it sounded a bit far-fetched, but I gathered it was more the volume of sound he was concerned about. He wanted them to be heard over a long distance.

DEF. COUN.: By anyone in particular?

BARNES: By as many people as possible, sir.

DEF. COUN.: He was teaching them to sing, wasn't he, Sergeant?

BARNES: That was his intention, sir.

JUDGE: To do *what*?

DEF. COUN.: To sing, m'lord.

JUDGE: I thought we were talking about weighing machines?

DEF. COUN.: These are a special type, m'lord, which speak when subjected to weight and can also be trained to sing. I have had these three brought into the Court for this reason, m'lord. There would be no difficulty in arranging for them to sing a short song, or part of a song, if your lordship would allow.

JUDGE: How long is this going to take?

DEF. COUN.: It would take a matter of minutes, m'lord.

JUDGE: (*unenthusiastically*). Yes. I suppose so.

DEF. COUN.: I am very much obliged to your lordship.

Defending Counsel nods to Usher.

The Usher lifts a weight on to each of the three weighing machines in turn.

When all three weights have been placed in position, the Usher gives middle C on a whistle.

After a brief pause Numbers Two and Three launch into the Lizzie Borden song as a duet. Number One is silent.

The Judge, in so far as he takes notice of the song at all, remains unimpressed by it.

The song ends.

Pause.

DEF. COUN.: (*rising*). Thank you, m'lord.

The Usher removes the weight first from Two and then from Three.

DEF. COUN.: (*as Usher goes to remove the weight from Number One*). One final question, Sergeant Barnes.

NUMBER ONE: (*as weight is removed*). Fifteen stone ten pounds.

There is a pause for one puzzled moment.

DEF. COUN.: (*resuming*). Was anything said to you, Sergeant Barnes, either by the accused or by his parents, that might lead you to believe he was intending eventually to have these weighing machines shipped to the North Pole?

BARNES: Yes, sir. Arrangements were actually in hand for this, sir.

DEF. COUN.: Did he volunteer any information that might explain this action?

BARNES: Only to say that he wanted them to act as sirens, sir.

JUDGE: (*intervening*). Sirens?

BARNES: (*in an explanatory manner*). To lure people to the North Pole, m'lord.

DEF. COUN.: There was a scientific reason for this, Sergeant Barnes, wasn't there?

BARNES: Yes, sir.

DEF. COUN.: Will you try and enlarge on this for his lordship, Sergeant Barnes?

BARNES: (*to Judge*). I fancy he had some notion, m'lord, that once these people were at the North Pole, if he could get enough of them together in the one place, he would have very little difficulty in persuading them all to jump at the same moment.

JUDGE: And what inscrutable purpose was this manoeuvre calculated to serve?

BARNES: I think he was more concerned with what would happen when they landed again, m'lord. He was hoping it might have the effect of tilting the earth's axis a little more to one side, m'lord.
Pause.

JUDGE: I see.

DEF. COUN.: This would very likely bring about quite far-reaching climatic changes, would it not, Sergeant?

BARNES: I think something of that kind was what he had in mind, sir.

DEF. COUN.: A shifting of the Ice Cap, for instance.

BARNES: Yes, sir.

DEF. COUN.: This might well give rise to a new Ice Age so far as these islands are concerned?

BARNES: In all probability, yes, sir.

DEF. COUN.: Would it be true to say, Sergeant Barnes, that he was hoping in this way to provide himself with a self-perpetuating pretext for wearing black?

BARNES: Yes, sir.

DEF. COUN.: By ensuring that for an indefinite period deaths from various causes connected with the excessive cold would be many and frequent?

BARNES: That was at the back of it, yes, sir.

DEF. COUN.: Thank you, Sergeant Barnes.
Barnes stands down.

DEF. COUN.: I would like to call Mrs. Groomkirby now to the witness box. (*To Usher.*) Mrs. Groomkirby?

USHER: Mrs. Groomkirby!

POLICEMAN: Mrs. Groomkirby!

MRS. G.: (*off*). Give me time to get downstairs. (*Appearing from hall.*) Where do I go?

She is shown into the witness box.

MRS. G.: You feel so public.

*In the witness box Mrs. Groomkirby becomes
somewhat overawed by her surroundings.
She takes the oath.*

DEF. COUN.: You are Mabel Laurentina Groomkirby.

MRS. G.: Yes, sir.

DEF. COUN.: You are the mother of the accused, Mrs. Groomkirby are you not?

MRS. G.: Oh. Well, yes. I suppose if he's on trial I must
be. I hadn't realized.

DEF. COUN.: It would be true to say, wouldn't it, Mrs. Groomkirby, that your son likes wearing black?

MRS. G.: He's worn it all his life.

DEF. COUN.: He likes wearing black but he doesn't feel justified
in wearing it except at the funeral of someone he
knows?

MRS. G.: Well, it's only in the last few years he's come to
think like that, really. He always used to just
wear it.

DEF. COUN.: His attitude has changed?

MRS. G.: It's been very noticeable over the last year or two.

DEF. COUN.: Can you account for this change in any way, Mrs.
Groomkirby?

MRS. G.: Not really—unless his studies have had anything
to do with it. He's always been of a very logical
turn of mind ever since he was born, but what
with all this studying lately he seems to have got
a different attitude altogether these last few years.

DEF. COUN.: Your son is a rather ingenious young man, is he
not, Mrs. Groomkirby?

MRS. G.: A lot of people say he is, yes, sir.

DEF. COUN.: He has a cash register, I believe.

MRS. G.: That's right.

DEF. COUN.: What exactly is the function of this cash register,
Mrs. Groomkirby? What does your son use it
for?

MRS. G.: It was an egg-timer to begin with, and then he

gradually came to rely on it more and more for other things.

DEF. COUN.: When it was an egg-timer—can you tell his lordship how it worked?

MRS. G.: Well, sir, it was rigged up in the kitchen with the telephone on one side of it and the gas stove on the other. He likes to have his eggs done the exact time—just the four minutes ten seconds—or he won't eat them. He just goes right inside himself. So he rigged up the cash register.

DEF. COUN.: How did it work, Mrs. Groomkirby?

MRS. G.: He'd got a stop-watch but he wouldn't trust that. He'd trust it for the minutes but he wouldn't trust it for the seconds.

DEF. COUN.: And so he used the cash register instead?

MRS. G.: That and the telephone. He had them side by side.

DEF. COUN.: What was the actual procedure he adopted, Mrs. Groomkirby?

MRS. G.: Well, he'd put his egg on to boil, then he'd stand there with his stop-watch.

DEF. COUN.: Go on, Mrs. Groomkirby.

MRS. G.: Well, then the moment it said four minutes exactly on his stop-watch, he'd simply dial TIM, wait for the pips, ring up No Sale on the cash register and take out his egg.

DEF. COUN.: And this was, in fact, the only sequence of actions that took precisely the ten seconds?

MRS. G.: That's right, sir. He wouldn't eat them otherwise.

DEF. COUN.: And he worked this out for himself without any assistance whatever from anyone else?

MRS. G.: Oh, yes. It was entirely his own. And then he started getting dependent on the bell for other things as well. Eating first; and now practically everything he does he has to have a bell rung.

DEF. COUN.: To come back to this question of the black clothes, Mrs. Groomkirby.

MRS. G.: They've as good as told him that if ever he were

87

to part with his cash register it would mean total paralysis for him.

DEF. COUN.: Yes. You say your son, Mrs. Groomkirby, has always liked wearing black. Will you tell his lordship in your own words about this attachment to black clothes?

MRS. G.: Well, sir, all his baby things were black. He had a black shawl and rompers and even down to his bib were all black, and his sheets and pillow-cases. We had everything in black for him as soon as he was born. People used to stop in the street and remark about him. He's never worn anything white. Sometimes when he was in his pram people used to say he looked like a wee undertaker lying there. We got it all planned before he was born that if we had a white baby we were going to dress him in black—or her in black if it had been a girl—and if either of them were black we'd have everything white, so as to make a contrast. But when he came he was white so we had the black.

JUDGE: (*intervening*). Is your husband a coloured man, Mrs. Groomkirby?

MRS. G.: He's an insurance agent, sir.

JUDGE: Yes, but is he coloured?

MRS. G.: Well, no, sir. Not so far as I know.

JUDGE: What I'm trying to get from you, Mrs. Groomkirby, is the simple fact of your husband's racial characteristics. Does he, for instance, have any negro blood?

MRS. G.: Well—he *has* got one or two bottles up in his room, but he doesn't tell me what's *in* them.
The Judge looks blankly at Mrs. Groomkirby for a moment and then relinquishes the matter.

DEF. COUN.: There's one more thing I should like to ask you, Mrs. Groomkirby. Each of your son's forty-three victims was struck with an iron bar after having been told a joke. Would it be true to say that

88

your son, Mrs. Groomkirby, went to considerable trouble over these jokes?

MRS. G.: He went to very great trouble indeed, sir. He sat up to all hours thinking out jokes for them.

DEF. COUN.: Can you tell his lordship why your son went to all this trouble with every one of his forty-three victims, when there were a number of far simpler methods he could have used?

MRS. G.: I think for one thing he rather took to the humorous side of it. And for another thing he always wanted to do everything he could for these people. He felt very sorry for them.

DEF. COUN.: He wanted to make things as pleasant as possible for them even at some considerable trouble and inconvenience to himself?

MRS. G.: He didn't mind how much trouble he went to, as long as they ended on a gay note.

DEF. COUN.: Thank you, Mrs. Groomkirby.

Mrs. Groomkirby is invited by a sign from the Usher to stand down and does so with respectful restraint.

Once out of the aura of the Court, and in her own home, she resumes a brisker manner and picking up the tray goes into the kitchen with it.

Counsel for the Defence begins his speech to the Judge.

DEF. COUN.: M'lord, in asking you to take a lenient view of this case, I am not underestimating the seriousness of the offences this young man has committed. They are very grave breaches of the law, and no one realizes this now more than he does himself. He has made very considerable efforts to find other ways of satisfying this—in itself quite harmless, indeed laudable—desire for a logical pretext, but so far, unfortunately, he has met with little success. He has had this scheme involving the weighing machines. We may think this to have been a somewhat grandiose scheme and that there

89

could be very little hope of its succeeding, or even indeed of its being universally acceptable were it possible to adopt it; the important thing is that it has been worked out by this astonishingly resourceful and gifted young man as the result of a determination to avoid by every means in his power any further breach of the law in satisfying this craving he has for black clothes. He has gone to very great trouble and expense in training these weighing machines, m'lord, with the intention not of sitting idly down beside them to listen to and enjoy the fruits of his labours himself, but of keeping himself indirectly from coming into conflict with the law. In my respectful submission, m'lord, this very complex personality with whom we are dealing is not in any ordinary sense of the word a killer; he is, on the contrary, a kindly, rather gentle young man, not given to violence— except in this one respect—and showing himself to be quite exceptionally considerate of others even to the extent of arranging, at considerable personal sacrifice of time and energy, for them to die laughing. I would therefore ask your lordship to pass as light a sentence as, in your lordship's judgment, is warranted in this very exceptional case.

Defending Counsel sits.

Kirby appears, looking for Gormless. He checks on seeing Gormless and raises his baton.

The Judge addresses the accused.

Kirby drops to his knees facing the Judge.

JUDGE: There have been too many crimes of this nature: people killing a number of victims—forty-three in your case—from what appear to be, and indeed often are in themselves, laudable motives. Your counsel has made an eloquent plea for you, and two people have been willing to come into the witness box—one of them the detective who arrested you—and give a favourable account of you. But from your forty-three victims—not a word. Not one of those forty-three has felt under any obligation to come forward and speak for you, notwithstanding the great trouble we are told you went to in furnishing them with laughing matter. And what about the iron bar you used? Was this also chosen and wielded with the well-being of your victims in mind? I think not. Your mother has said that you wear black. This is not surprising. Such a taste seems to me to be in perfect conformity with the career you have chosen to embark upon. I am not greatly influenced by the reasons that have been put forward for your having this apparently irresistible craving—they seem to me to have very little bearing on the matter. It is becoming more and more an accepted feature of cases of this kind that in the course of them the court is subjected to a farrago of psychological poppycock in which every imaginable ailment in the nursery is prayed in aid. As for your desire to find a logical pretext, this is the one redeeming feature I have been able to find in this case. But you could have come by a pretext in any one of a number of quite legitimate ways. I have no doubt at all that at least a score of undertakers could have been found whose advice and assistance you could have had for the asking. Instead you chose another way, a way which has led you straight to this court. You began a few months ago by telling your first joke to your first victim and then striking him with an iron bar. What did you get out of it? The excuse to wear black for a day or two. Was it really worth breaking the law in order to be able to wear black for forty-eight hours? And then a little later on came your second murder, and the opportunity to wear black again for a short time. And so it has gone on: victim after victim, until even you could not have expected the authorities to overlook it any longer. Indeed Detective-Sergeant Barnes warned you quite explicitly what would happen if you broke the law for the forty-fourth time. There seems to me to be not the smallest shred of excuse for these repeated offences. As for this diabolical scheme to send weighing machines to the North Pole, which we have been told is so ingenious, the less said about it the better. If the song we have just had to listen to in this court is in any way typical of the kind of thing we were to have been regaled by from the North Pole, it would be hard to imagine what sort of person would have been enticed there by it—or having got there would want to remain for long within earshot, still less be in any fit state to jump up and down. In deciding upon the sentence I shall impose in this case, I have been influenced by one consideration, and it is this: that in sentencing a man for one crime, we may be putting him beyond the reach of the law in respect of those other crimes of which he might otherwise have become guilty. The law, however, is not to be cheated in this way. I shall therefore discharge you.

Mrs. Groomkirby enters from the hall on the last words of the Judge and rings up No Sale on the cash register.

This is the signal for a massed choir to launch into the Hallelujah Chorus, and for blackout of the Court and living-room.

Kirby flings out his arms to conduct choir.

Each alternate Hallelujah is sung by Gormless who is now lit up with the words 'I speak your weight' in red.

Gormless takes over from the massed choir, Kirby in a mood of ungainly gaiety conducts him, and finally, when Gormless relapses into silence takes out a

92

*weight and crossing the forestage with it conducts
and accompanies its tiny piping treble in a gay
childlike rendering of the same Hallelujah Chorus.
He goes off Left.*
The light comes up on the living-room.
*The Court is empty. Mrs. Groomkirby is dusting it.
Sylvia is sitting as at the beginning of ACT ONE
in silence.*

MRS. G.: (*with a nod towards the music stand which remains
where Kirby placed it*). What's that doing down
here?
Pause.

MRS. G.: You might take it up, Sylvia.

SYLVIA: (*looking up*). Take what up?

MRS. G.: (*going out to kitchen*). That thing whatever it is of
Kirby's. It's no business being down here.

SYLVIA: Can't he come and get it himself?

MRS. G.: (*off*). You know very well he's busy up there,
Sylvia.
*Sylvia shrugs, goes on reading for a moment, then
puts her magazine down and saunters out with the
music stand.*
*Barnes appears from the forestage Left. He is getting
into his overcoat and calls somewhat defensively to
Mrs. Groomkirby.*

BARNES: Thank you, Mrs. Groomkirby.
*Mrs. Groomkirby enters from the kitchen with a tray
of food which she sets out on the table as for Mrs.
Gantry.*

MRS. G.: Just off, are you?

BARNES: Yes—they've had a good look round and . . .
Sylvia enters from the hall and sits with magazine.

MRS. G.: (*without looking up from her work*). Seen all they
want, have they?

BARNES: I think they have, yes. More or less. (*Edging off.*)

MRS. G.: (*half to herself*). Day in day out. Gawping. The
place isn't your own.

BARNES: (*escaping*). Back tomorrow about half past seven

then, Mrs. Groomkirby—if that's all right.

MRS. G.: They won't have to come expecting anything.

BARNES: I'll tell them. Good-bye, Mrs. Groomkirby. Good-bye, Sylvia. (*Barnes goes off.*)

Mr. Groomkirby enters from the hall and crosses the stage slowly with a book open in his hand. He has on the Judge's wig and robe. Neither seems to be made for him.

SYLVIA: (*without looking up*). I don't know why they don't all go and stand outside Buckingham Palace or something instead.

MR. G.: (*trying out what he thinks may be an appropriate voice and manner as he reads. At large*). That, members of the jury, is the evidence before you. *Dissatisfied, he moves further right and takes up one or two tentative stances.*

SYLVIA: Or the Taj Mahal or something. And gawp at that, instead.

MR. G.: (*in an undertone*). That, members of the jury . . . *He abandons it and tries again.*

AUNT M.: On roller-skates. By moonlight. To Outer Space!

MR. G.: (*he has got it right and addresses Gormless without recognition as though speaking to the Foreman of the jury*). That, members of the jury, is the evidence before you. (*He turns to go, delivering his final words in a dismissively offhand manner.*) What weight you give to it is a matter entirely for you.

GORMLESS: (*lighting up*). Fifteen stone ten pounds.

The sound stops Mr. Groomkirby in his tracks. He turns, startled, puzzled, deflated in turn. He goes hopelessly off.

CURTAIN